T3-BNW-598

The Censors and the Schools

The Censors and the Schools

by

Jack Nelson *and* Gene Roberts, Jr.

GREENWOOD PRESS, PUBLISHERS
WESTPORT, CONNECTICUT

Library of Congress Cataloging in Publication Data

Nelson, Jack, 1929 (Oct. 11)-
The censors and the schools.

Reprint of the 1st ed. published by Little, Brown, Boston.
Includes bibliographies.
1. Text-books--United States. 2. Pressure groups--United States. I. Roberts, Gene, joint author. II. Title.
[LB3047.N44 1977] 371.32 77-23390
ISBN 0-8371-9687-6

Originally published in 1963 by Little, Brown and Company, Boston

Reprinted by permission of Little, Brown and Company

Reprinted in 1977 by Greenwood Press, Inc.

Library of Congress Catalog Card Number 77-23390

ISBN 0-8371-9687-6

Printed in the United States of America

To

Frank Freidel
Theodore Morrison
Arthur Schlesinger, Sr.

Acknowledgments

In 1961–1962, while we were at Harvard University under the Nieman Fellowship program for newspapermen, Professor of History Frank Freidel suggested that we investigate the activities of pressure groups which attempt to influence the selection and contents of textbooks. We planned a magazine article. But it soon became apparent that our findings would be much too extensive for that purpose. We found a wealth of material about a serious problem which, although it affects every public school in the country, has been given little attention by the nation's news media and magazines. We found that few books have been written on the subject. Our research indicated none in the past quarter of a century.

We gratefully acknowledge the encouragement and advice of Frank Freidel and two other Harvard professors — Theodore Morrison and Arthur Schlesinger, Sr., both of whom carefully read the manuscript, made many suggestions and contributed greatly to the final product.

Our richest source of research material was in the offices

of the Commission on Professional Rights and Responsibilities of the National Education Association in Washington, D.C. We are especially indebted to Richard Barnes Kennan, executive secretary of the Commission, and Edwin W. Davis, associate secretary, and their staff members for making their files available to us and offering many suggestions.

Several Nieman Fellows of the 1961–1962 Class criticized our work and aided in some of the research. They include: Peter Binzen, education editor, the Philadelphia *Bulletin;* David Kraslow, Washington correspondent of the Knight Newspapers; John O. Emmerich, managing editor of the McComb, Mississippi, *Enterprise-Journal;* John Hamilton, associate editor of the Lynchburg, Virginia, *News;* and Jim Mathis, Washington correspondent of the Houston *Post.*

For aid on research in Mississippi we are indebted to John N. Herbers, Jr., of Jackson, state manager of United Press International. In Texas we were greatly assisted by Editor Willie Morris and Associate Editor Robert Sherrill, both of the *Texas Observer* in Austin, and J. Frank Dobie, author. Robert Skaife, executive secretary of the Affiliated Teachers Organizations of Los Angeles, helped us in California.

Dr. Erling M. Hunt, Professor of History at Teachers College, Columbia University, who has collected information on attacks on textbooks for the past thirty years, made available to us part of a report on the subject he was preparing in 1962 for the American Historical Association and the Mississippi Valley Historical Association. Dr. Hunt advised us as to the major developments in textbook controversies in the past.

Our coverage of the textbook battle in Meriden, Connecticut, would not have been nearly so complete without the assistance of Warren F. Gardner, editor of the Meriden *Record,* and Editor Sanford H. Wendover of the Meriden *Journal.*

Several publishing companies, especially D. C. Heath, Ginn and Company, Houghton Mifflin, and McGraw-Hill, were of invaluable assistance. Officials of each company freely discussed censorship problems facing the industry and welcomed open discussion of the attacks on textbooks.

We also appreciate the many others, too numerous to mention (including several Nieman Fellows), who helped us check out information throughout the country. And we owe a special thanks to Louis Lyons, curator of the Nieman Foundation, and to his wife, Totty. We depended upon Louis for advice and counsel and upon Totty for the basics such as locating office space and typewriters, steering us to sources of information and promising from the outset to "buy the first copy."

We can't, of course, begin to thank our wives, Virginia Nelson and Susan Roberts, for their constant encouragement.

Contents

The Censors and the Schools

1

Anatomy of a Textbook Crisis

ON NOVEMBER 24, 1961, the residents of Meriden, Connecticut, were shocked to learn they had been accused of financing the subversion of their own schoolchildren. They were not called Communist conspirators, but were considered dupes. Under a three-column headline on page one the evening *Journal* told the story: Two citizens named Casey and Dobson had charged that textbooks used in Meriden's two public high schools were "brainwashing" the students.

Like most attacks on textbooks, the charges came without warning. And to a city that prides itself upon its patriotism, a city that still honors the men it lost in the Revolutionary War, they came as a jolt. During World War II, the Federal War Manpower Commission designated Meriden as "the Nation's Ideal War Community." For its efforts in converting its factories to war production, it also was selected as the setting for a morale-boosting movie, "Main Street Today," filmed by Metro-Goldwyn-Mayer.

Meriden had grown under the free-enterprise system from a colonial farm of "ye number of 200 acres of upland

and 50 acres of meadow" to a prospering industrial city of 52,000. The Chamber of Commerce proudly labeled Meriden the "Silver City" in honor of its leading industry, International Silver Co., the nation's largest producer of household silverware.

Never before had the city been caught up in a controversy over Communism. And it had been free of textbook battles for half a century. In 1911, a citizens' committee urged school officials to "eliminate the study of Shakespeare's *Merchant of Venice* from the curricula of Meriden schools." The committee, composed both of Jews and Gentiles, said the play and its chief character – the Jewish usurer Shylock – fanned hatred against the Jewish people. Shylock was regarded by the committee as a "grossly exaggerated caricature of anything human." The committee won its fight.

The *Merchant of Venice* controversy originated locally. The 1961 charges did not. Like most of the modern attacks on textbooks, they were sparked by propaganda from a national organization. They germinated in the Washington headquarters of the Daughters of the American Revolution. There, in the white marble building in the fall of 1960, a clerk mailed a twenty-page pamphlet. The envelope carried this address: Edward Casey, 85 Liberty Street, Meriden, Conn.

A few days later Casey, a thirty-one-year-old purchasing agent for the Pratt and Whitney Aircraft Corporation, drove his green MG sports car to the old remodeled hilltop home he shares with his parents. He found the envelope waiting. The parcel was unsolicited; he received it because, as a subscriber to the *National Defender,* a DAR publication, he was put on the Daughters' mailing list. Casey had frequently brooded because of what he felt was widespread subversion in this country, and he eagerly read the pamphlet, entitled *Textbook Study*.

It was an alarming report. A DAR committee had examined 220 public-school books and blacklisted 170 of them for being "subversive." Only 50 of the books met "minimum DAR standards." The names of the authors of the condemned texts read like rosters of the American Historical Association and other social-science organizations.

What was wrong with the books? "Unfortunately there is a perceivable pattern of 'economic determinism' running through the unsatisfactory texts on all subjects," according to the *Textbook Study*. "History books and economics texts contain uncomplimentary pictures of slum areas or of long lines of the unemployed during 'The Great Depression,' one book even labeling such a photograph 'A Long Line of Unemployed Waiting for Christmas Dinners.' "

The Daughters also suggested that stress given such subjects as tolerance, bigotry, prejudice and mental health pointed to "some central source within the educational apparatus" which was dictating what the books must emphasize.

They also disliked the attention given to "internationalism" and the United Nations. And the word "democracy" caused grave concern: "It is characteristic of the social science approach to history that while the government of the United States is described as a 'democracy' and seldom as a representative Republic, Soviet Russia and China are scrupulously called 'republics.' " The Daughters objected that music books contained "too many 'work tunes' and 'folk songs' (as distinguished from native and national airs)."

In the supplemental reading lists of the textbooks the Daughters found the names of "liberals and internationalists" included among the authors. They objected to students reading books by such persons as Theodore H. White, Margaret Mead, Burl Ives, Lincoln Steffens, Louis Untermeyer, Richard Wright, Bill Mauldin, Langston Hughes, Carey McWilliams and Gordon Allport. "The records of these persons," said the Daughters, "are available from the House Committee on Un-American Activities upon the request of your Congressman." Historians such as Henry Steele Commager, Herbert Agar, Harold Laski and Allan Nevins, former president of the American Historical Association, who wrote the foreword to President Kennedy's *Profiles in Courage,* were included in the pamphlet's list of "liberal, racial, socialist or labor agitators."

The *Textbook Study* urged that its readers obtain "a copy of the official textbook list in your community. Check it against the DAR list of satisfactory and unsatisfactory books." Readers were warned, "It will take courage to pursue this course. You will be challenging the 'entrenched liberal' position. You will find there is no one so intolerant or vindictive as the 'liberal' who is quick to deny freedom of speech if it includes criticism of the propaganda in textbooks."

The warning only served to stimulate Casey's interest. When he put aside the pamphlet, he was convinced there was "subversion" in the classroom. He was indignant and ready to do battle.

It would be no small task to check all the social studies books used in the two high schools, and Casey looked for someone to help him – someone he could trust. He decided on an old friend, Frederick H. Dobson, an expediter, also employed by Pratt and Whitney Aircraft.

Ed Casey had met Fred Dobson, who was seventeen years older, in the early fifties when one of Fred's sons was a Boy Scout and Ed a scoutmaster in a troop sponsored by St. Rose Roman Catholic Church. Through the years they saw each other occasionally at the aircraft plant and at Holy Name Society functions. Both were past presidents of the society.

In 1959 they became close political friends, campaigning together for the election of a Meriden merchant, John Ivers, as mayor. After Iver's election, Casey became a Republican committeeman for the city and Dobson was appointed to the city Board of Apportionment and Taxation. Both were dedicated to "converting the liberal Republican Party in Connecticut into a conservative party." At the suggestion of Mayor Ivers, whom they regarded as a "good ultra-conservative," they began reading right-wing periodicals like the *Dan Smoot Report* and *Human Events,* both of which have warned against subversion in books.

In some respects Casey and Dobson were strikingly different. Both wore black horn-rimmed glasses, but there the physical similarities ended. Casey was tall and slim, a nice-looking bachelor who liked to wear colorful sport shirts and tilted his hat at an angle. Dobson, who had four children, was of medium height and rather pudgy, a distinguished-looking man with wavy gray hair, a conservative dresser. Casey participated in amateur theatricals, and he frequently drove the ninety miles from Meriden to New York City to attend meetings of the Young Americans for Freedom, a political-action organization whose National Advisory Board members include at least six textbook reviewers for national propaganda agencies. Casey studied at Georgetown University in Washington, but later transferred to the University of Connecticut, from which he was graduated. Dobson was too old to be a Young American for Freedom, but he sometimes drove with Casey to the New York meetings. He was interested in education and once served on the municipal library board, but he had not attended college. Dobson was determined that his children should go to college, but he worried that they might become "liberals" in the process of getting their degrees.

When Casey showed Dobson the DAR's *Textbook Study,* the older man gasped at the charges. He shook his head. "This can't be happening in Meriden," he said. But he quickly agreed to help Casey investigate.

The two men obtained a list of the twenty-nine social studies books in use in Maloney and Platt high schools. A comparison with the blacklisted books in *Textbook Study* confirmed their worst fears: fourteen of the local books were among the condemned. What made it appear even worse was the fact that only two of the schools' books were on the "satisfactory list"; thirteen had not been mentioned at all in the DAR report. Fourteen out of sixteen were on the blacklist!

"I wouldn't have believed it," exclaimed Dobson. "But here it is right before us!"

Several months later, over a cup of coffee in a downtown Meriden restaurant, Casey and Dobson told one of the authors of this book that they worked long and hard on their lengthy report condemning the Meriden textbooks.

"We decided that we just couldn't rush into this thing, even though the DAR disapproved of so many of the books,"

Casey said. "We had to take our time and be sure of our facts. You have to be careful what you say about liberals. For example, you can't say Eleanor Roosevelt is a Communist. You just say she's leaning in the pinko direction."

Until he began checking, Casey said, he had no idea that so many organizations were active in sending out material on Red-tainted textbooks. He soon found that he had a book rack full of pamphlets and booklets telling about the Communist conspiracy to win the minds of American children, especially through subtle subversion in books.

Dobson, who had been quietly sipping his coffee and listening to Casey, was more interested in talking about how they had been "smeared" than how subversive they had found the texts. "We're not members of the John Birch Society," he said, "but we're always being accused of it. We've been accused of being book burners, but that's not true."

"We're just ultra-conservatives," Casey interjected. "We're not the fanatics of the right you read so much about."

"If you ask me," Dobson volunteered, "the attacks on the far right are Communist tactics. They did the same thing to Senator McCarthy, they smeared him."

"But about the report on the textbooks," said Dobson. "We were only doing our duty, but we worked hard and documented our charges. And when we finished we dug into our own pockets for money and had the report mimeographed. We could only afford about two hundred copies, but we sent them where we thought they would do the most good — to members of the school board and the newspapers and the library and to some other people."

Casey and Dobson had no trouble locating source material

to be used in condemning the Meriden books. Mrs. Wilson K. Barnes, who was then chairman of the National Defense Committee of the DAR, provided them with additional information and references. They found other organizations willing and even eager to give them assistance.

They received a copy of a thirteen-year-old report called *A Bill of Grievances* from the Sons of the American Revolution. From America's Future, Inc., in New Rochelle, New York, they obtained a series of textbook reviews. America's Future also provided them with a copy of *What's Happened to Our Schools* by Rosalie M. Gordon, who once attacked the U. S. Supreme Court in another booklet entitled, *Nine Men Against America.* By sending a dollar to the Institute of Special Research at Box 20220 in Pasadena, California, Casey and Dobson got another pamphlet, *The Left Swing in Education.* They also purchased a copy of *Brainwashing in the High Schools* by E. Merrill Root, a small-college English professor turned critic of "subversive" textbooks. A thick report on textbooks came from the Florida Coalition of Patriotic Societies. The Parents for Better Education in Los Angeles, California, sent a detailed system for rating textbooks. Old American Legion resolutions and statements proved useful.

When their stack of literature on textbooks was knee-high, Casey and Dobson began sifting through it, lifting quotations and references for use in their attack on the Meriden schoolbooks. They worked on the project at nights and on weekends and whenever they had a spare moment.

The report was completed in November, 1961, a year after Casey first read the DAR pamphlet. So quietly had they gone about their task that only their families and close friends had been aware of their project. Local school officials were to complain later that the two critics had never consulted them about the books before making their charges public. And Casey and Dobson refused to say how they obtained a list of the books used in Meriden schools — a list they could have obtained by merely requesting it from school officials.

The neatly typed thirty-page document, which newspapers called "The Casey-Dobson Report," came quickly to the point: "After a careful examination of the social science texts . . . the conclusion is reached that Meriden parents are indeed financing the 'subversion' of their own children in their own public schools." The report defined subversion as anything tending to undermine "faith and allegiance."

Like the DAR, Casey and Dobson were angered by the attention given the United Nations in the textbooks. And they contended that the name of every author should be followed by a list of any House Un-American Activities Committee citations he might have accumulated. Their report was sprinkled with passages from the literature and correspondence they had collected.

They quoted Rudolf K. Scott, president of America's Future, Inc., as saying: "Many factors have contributed to the startling fact that our schools are turning out young people who have no faith in our system of American Constitutional Government and our free enterprise economy, but the single most important factor has been the slanted textbooks now in use in our schools, particularly in the social studies field."

Less than nine pages of the report were devoted to specific reviews of the books Casey and Dobson condemned. In almost every case the criticism was lifted from DAR material, *Brainwashing in the High Schools,* or the textbook reviews prepared by America's Future, Inc. A one-third-page criticism of the 1954 edition of *Making of Modern America* was typical of the Casey-Dobson complaints. They objected because the book suggested the student read selections from such authors as Stuart Chase, Louis Dolivet, Henry S. Commager and David S. Muzzey. They included a lengthy DAR comment that the book had a "socialist slant," as evidenced by such subtitles as "Panics and Depression Become More Severe"; "Industrialization Brings Problems as Well as Benefits"; and "Congress Attempts to Curb the Trusts."

Casey and Dobson also complained because books and articles by novelist Pearl Buck, magazine editor Norman Cousins and sixteen other authors were listed as recommended reading by some of the texts. Miss Buck, they said, had appealed for help "on behalf of the Russian peoples" in 1941 and had sponsored a dinner during World War II celebrating the twenty-fifth anniversary of the Red Army. And they charged that she had urged the lifting of the Spanish Embargo, had been a member of the advisory board of the Japanese-American Committee for Democracy and had been a sponsor of the Congress of American-Soviet Friendship. They listed some pamphlets and reports in which Cousins's name had been mentioned, but they gave no details.

The two critics sent copies of their report to the Meriden newspapers, and reporters for the morning *Record* immediately began placing telephone calls to Connecticut colleges and universities. They wanted to know if Connecticut historians and political scientists agreed that high-school textbooks should not make references to authors like Buck, Cousins and Commager.

Professor Joseph C. Palamountain, chairman of the Government Department at Wesleyan University, certainly did not agree: "If my child were going to the Meriden schools, I would think he would be shortchanged if he were not reading people like this."

Professor James Fesler, professor of political science at Yale, was indignant: "It is incredible to me that persons who have contributed so much to the intellectual life of America, the defense of American ideas and the thoughtful analysis of the challenges we face could be brought into question concerning the ideas that made America great."

Meriden's school leaders were quiet, but only for a day. Morton H. Greenblatt, a lawyer and chairman of the Meriden school board, triggered the opposition to Casey and Dobson twenty-four hours after their charges were published. "They have taken canned reports prepared by others far removed from Meriden," Greenblatt said, "and on the basis of quotations from these reports are attempting to cast aspersions on Meriden's schools. I further question the background of these men. I question whether they have the experience and qualifications that would enable them to undertake so important a project."

Each day that followed saw more Meriden residents choose sides in the controversy. The Rt. Rev. Msgr. Joseph M. Griffin, permanent rector of the church attended by Casey and Dobson and an influential figure among New England Roman Catholics, urged the critics to "stand firm" in their beliefs. He congratulated them for their "efforts to alert people to the dangers of not being alert."

Not all clergymen agreed with the Monsignor. A Baptist

minister, L. L. Larsen, declared: "When Pearl Buck, an author who has thrilled millions, and Norman Cousins, the distinguished editor of the *Saturday Review of Literature,* are branded as unfit for human consumption, what authors might the authors suggest?" Rabbi Albert N. Troy told an audience at Temple B'nai Abraham that the report "a-wakens us to the danger of the authoritarian point of view which those who made the report represent."

Parents as well as clergymen were caught up in the controversy. One housewife who followed the textbook developments closely was Mrs. Katherine G. Dorsey, the wife of a prominent Meriden attorney. In 1942, as a teacher freshly graduated from college, she had taught Edward Casey freshman English. "He was very, very quiet," she recalled twenty years later, "and a good student. He was at the top of the class I taught for students who were not taking pre-college courses. I don't know how he would have ranked had he been in the college group – a little above average I guess.".

Several years ago Mrs. Dorsey began reading newspaper accounts of Casey's work in local dramatics groups. Later, her former student's name began appearing in Meriden newspapers even more regularly, as a contributor of "letters to the editor." One letter, in March 1961, hinted at the coming textbook crisis. Casey wrote that he was disturbed by the National Congress of Parents and Teachers and its "utter lack of concern for the most crucial problem of our day – the cold war being waged in the classroom for the minds of our youth."

Mrs. Dorsey was disturbed by Edward Casey. In the heat of textbook controversy and with "apologies to James

Whitcomb Riley," she wrote a poem for the Meriden *Record:*

Little Eddie Casey came to our schools today
To clean our desks and lockers out and sweep the Reds away,
And shoo the pinkos off their perch wherever they may be.
He's bringing back the rod of Birch to chastise you and me.
He's checked the books. He's checked the walls and checked the chalk and ink.
Because he's very thorough and he thought they might be pink.
But don't you think we mind it; 'cause when his work is done
We set around the bookfires havin' lots of fun
A-listening to the witch-tales that Eddie tells about,
About the Birchers that'll get ya if ya don't watch out.

Denying any affiliation with the semi-secret John Birch Society, Casey and Dobson began organizing opposition to the fourteen texts they had brought under attack. One of Meriden's two DAR chapters, the Susan Carrington Clarke Chapter, was an early recruit to the textbook fight. Members of the Ruth Hart Chapter were not impressed by the Casey-Dobson charges. They prepared a statement critical of the textbook report, but ruled out releasing it to the press "in obedience to the direction of the national organization." However, a former regent of the Ruth Hart Chapter, Mrs. Helen Rader, decided the Meriden schools were her first concern. She told Meriden educators and the press that Casey and Dobson "have done more to subvert a free society than the combined contents of the fourteen unsatisfactory textbooks could ever accomplish." Post 45 of the American Legion also dashed the hopes of the textbook critics. "We do not go along with Casey or Dobson at all," said Post Commander Roland Barber, "and we want to make it clear that we do not."

Casey and Dobson next turned to the Meriden Board of Education, which has the authority under Connecticut law to accept or reject textbooks. The Citizens Anti-Communist League of Connecticut agreed to send some of its members to a board meeting to testify on Communism and "creeping socialism." But the chief witness for Casey and Dobson was to be the author of *Brainwashing in the High Schools.* They drove to E. Merrill Root's isolated farm home in Rhode Island to persuade him to join in their textbook fight.

Only hours before the school board hearing on December 17, Root called Casey to cancel his appearance. He was no longer young, he said, and he was reluctant to drive over icy roads. But he wanted to do his part because he was in sympathy with their cause. He knew Casey as an enthusiastic member of the Young Americans for Freedom, which Root served as a member of the National Advisory Board. "You can quote me as saying your report is distinguished, sound and accurate," Root told Casey. The retired professor said he was convinced that the fourteen controversial books tended to "glorify the social and welfare state — the delusion of collectivism which is the first step to Communism."

Root's cancellation distressed the textbook critics, but it was too late to postpone their meeting with the board. They walked into the meeting room lugging a book rack filled with the anti-textbook literature they had accumulated. With them were more than a dozen supporters, some from out of town.

Casey, young and aggressive, was clearly in control of the censorship efforts. But he deferred to his partner for the opening presentation.

Dobson, his face reflecting anguish, began not by criticizing the books, but by complaining that he and Casey had been unfairly attacked. "We have been smeared and ridiculed," he told the school board members, and, raising his voice, he cried: "This is the Red-fascist timetable!"

"We don't want to hear about the Red-fascist timetable," retorted Morton Greenblatt, the board chairman. "We want to hear about the Meriden textbooks."

Casey came to his friend's rescue. Taking the floor quickly, he said their report of subversion was well documented, and he exclaimed: "Patriotism has to permeate all our books and it has to be lived sincerely by both parent and teacher."

"It has been your intent to create the impression that we're subverting the youngsters," Greenblatt countered. "What prompted you to write this report?"

"Being a good patriotic American."

The board listened with patience but not without irritation as Casey continued his argument that his charges were supported by such organizations as the DAR and such authorities as E. Merrill Root.

Emmett Ruland of Stratford, testifying for Casey and Dobson, broadened the charges. Identifying himself as a high-school teacher and chairman of the education committee of the Anti-Communist Committee of Connecticut, Ruland warned the board of "subversion in the field of education." Communists had infiltrated Connecticut colleges and high schools, he said, and there were seventeen Communist cell organizations in the New Haven area. He cited "unpatriotic activities" at Wesleyan University, Yale University, Trinity College and the University of Connecticut.

(Wesleyan University later issued a statement in answer to Ruland: "President Kennedy has eloquently expressed the danger of self-appointed experts in the lunatic fringe whose definition of patriotism is so wholly foreign to American tradition, it would be a joke to apply them.")

Ruland went on to say, "Each year there are ten to fifty lectures with Marxist-Leninist theories given under the guise of cultural exchanges at each of the state's institutions. All of these high-sounding names of topics are used for the destruction of America and poisoning the minds of our youths." Getting in a plug for the Casey-Dobson report, he told the committee the DAR standards for judging textbooks were the best available.

Anti-censorship witnesses testified when the critics had completed their charges. John Berwick, an assistant school superintendent, said the fourteen textbooks cited in the report were being used in "ninety-nine per cent of the high schools throughout the nation," and had not been questioned as to subversive content by qualified educators.

"That's a shame," Casey shot back.

Dr. George Magrath, superintendent of schools, said the teachers and the school system were dedicated to teaching Americanism and he resented any implication that they were brainwashing the students. Miss Claire Carter, assistant principal at Platt High School, defended the books and said they pointed out the evils of Communism. Miss Eleanor Dossin, citizenship teacher at Platt, said she deeply resented being accused of subverting the students. And William Papallo, history teacher at Maloney High School, said the "blanket indictment" of the school system had "upset" him and other teachers.

The school board was equally unimpressed by the report. Greenblatt told newsmen: "I am sure we will continue to use the books."

Meanwhile, the editor of the Meriden *Journal* was writing what he hoped would be an obituary for the textbook hassle. Editor Sanford H. Wendover could hardly be accused of being "subversive" or even a liberal. He is a conservative, and he frequently runs columns on his editorial page by such dedicated anti-liberals as George E. Sokolsky and Senator Barry Goldwater. But Wendover had no sympathy for the textbook criticism.

"Over the last weekend," he wrote, "we did a little personal research in the material contained in the textbooks. In an effort to discover whether or not the Casey-Dobson critique was founded on solid ground, we examined nine of the textbooks under fire. In our opinion, they are good textbooks—much better than the textbooks on American history and government we studied when we were in school. . . . The Casey-Dobson criticism seems to boil down to this: these books do not try to force extreme rightist sentiments upon high school students. For that matter, they do not attempt to make socialists or communists of them. Naturally each book interprets American history and politics from the viewpoint of its author or authors. Every writer puts something of himself into what he writes. Through the tables of reference, a historian tells his readers where to find other viewpoints and additional information. The student who pursues knowledge to its sources in this way is in no danger of being subverted."

A vigilant press, and education officials who were willing to take a strong stand, and at least two local patriotic organizations which were not beguiled by the "canned reports" from other states, quickly extinguished the censorship fire in Meriden before it came near the book-burning stage. But in other parts of the country alarmists have succeeded in preventing the adoption of certain books and in forcing alteration of others. Especially was this true beginning in 1958. From the early part of that year until the end of 1962, textbooks came under fire in nearly a third of the legislatures, in states as far apart as Illinois, Texas, Wisconsin and Florida.

In 1961 and 1962 the censorship groups accelerated their efforts. Their successes and the proliferation of right-wing groups to distribute their propaganda loomed as portents of even more activities in 1963 and after.

No state escapes the effects of the attacks on textbooks. Book censors in one state will force a publisher to alter a textbook and that book is sold, as altered, in other states. But more important, perhaps, is the impact the widespread attacks have on the textbook publishers, who are highly competitive. Publishers themselves acknowledge they must walk a narrow path to avoid controversy and offending any special interest groups. As a result, many books lack vitality and are too dull to interest the students. They treat controversial subjects superficially or not at all.

Where the censors scored best they operated in a vacuum. They escaped comprehensive coverage by the press and they met little organized opposition. In some instances conservative newspapers editorially acquiesced in, or even supported, censorship efforts. At the same time, the groups attacking textbooks were well organized and well financed, and they put up a solid front for their views.

The censors had different axes to grind, but they all found a common cause in the Communist menace, and managed to associate with it everything else they feared or hated. A segregationist in the South who equated integration with Communism gladly included the income tax, social security, organized labor and all the other hobgoblins of the rightists' lexicon in the same category. The Northern industrialist, who saw the hidden hand of the enemy in federal taxes and control of business, was willing to ascribe the same danger to the Supreme Court decisions which outlawed segregation. Communism was the culprit for physicians worried about socialized medicine, ministers troubled by "obscenities," and ordinary citizens concerned that the patriotism of other citizens was not up to par.

In Texas and Mississippi the censors forced legislative investigations to root out "subversion" in textbooks, and in both states the censors succeeded in altering the contents of some books and in killing the adoption of other texts.

Following a campaign by the DAR, the state Farm Bureau Federation, the White Citizens Council and the state American Legion, the Mississippi legislature voted to put the selection of textbooks virtually in the hands of its governor, Ross Barnett, a staunch segregationist.

In Texas, scholars described as "shameful" the extent to which the state Textbook Committee and publishers of schoolbooks bowed to the demands of censorship groups. And the Legislature adopted a platitudinous resolution providing for an investigation which was supposed to be aimed at books, but which found many other targets in a wild witch-hunt. Before it had ended, textbook authors and publishers, college professors and even anti-censorship legislators had been accused as willing conspirators or dupes of the Communists.

In California, home of several organizations which produce propaganda for nationwide attacks on schoolbooks, numerous textbook battles erupted, resulting in substantial changes in some books. In one case a California publishing house deleted an entire chapter on the United Nations from an eighth-grade civics text.

The mushrooming attacks on textbooks also took their toll in school libraries. Hundreds of books were withdrawn from library shelves in states from coast to coast. The American Book Publishers Council, Inc., reported that in 1961 alone, censorship groups attacked texts and school library books in at least eighteen states. The Council, in its March, 1962, *Freedom-To-Read Bulletin,* declared:

> While the same veterans' groups and venerable-lineage societies are still in the foreground in attacking textbooks, they have been joined in recent years by such newer bodies as the White Citizens Councils, the John Birch Society and the incredibly named National Indignation Convention. The attacks by organizations in this category are usually characterized by such pejorative phrases as "pro-New Deal," "pro-UN," "soft on communism" and variants thereof. An otherwise unassailable textbook will suffer because one of its co-authors had signed a petition, for example, in behalf of medical aid to Loyalist Spain or had openly contributed money to Russian War Relief amidst the snows of yesteryear.

While today's textbook battles are among the most widespread and serious ever to hit this country, they are not without deep roots in history.

2

The Past Is Prologue

THE MEMBERS of the American Historical Association were angry at critics who called the nation's textbooks un-American. "The clearly implied charges that many of our leading scholars are engaged in treasonable propaganda," the historians declared in a formal resolution, ". . . is inherently and obviously absurd."

These words could have been written in 1962; actually they were written in December, 1923, almost forty years earlier. Then, as now, critics thought they detected a conspiracy to subvert the nation's children, but their fears were directed not toward the Kremlin, but toward London. Men like Charles Grant Miller, who lambasted textbooks in a series of articles for the Hearst newspapers, were charging almost daily that school histories "have been revised and in some instances wholly rewritten in a new and propitiatory spirit toward England."

The targets of textbook censorship campaigns change from generation to generation, and so do the characters in the censorship drama. In one era, Civil War veterans, some of them with battle wounds, shouted that textbooks were undermining the causes which they carried into battle at Shiloh, Bull Run, Gettysburg. One year the censor will be the businessman in fashionable Homburg and delicately tailored suit, demanding that children be taught the evils of municipal systems of power distribution. The next, trade unionists in shirtsleeves will be seeking to write the "labor viewpoint" into the texts. The censor may be the frail grandmother who fingers her cameo brooch as she tells the local school board that every book should warn the child of the perils of strong drink. Again, the book assailant may be a stern fundamentalist who frets that evolutionist teaching will damn his child to Hell; or it may be the racist who finds something menacing in talk of brotherhood and equality of races.

Whatever their differences in dress or the nature of their worries, would-be textbook censors share the same convictions: that their views are the correct ones, that the child will be subverted if he hears an opposing philosophy. Always, the censors ignore the fact that no textbook can ever be perfect, and that textbooks will always reflect the changing knowledge and the changing interpretations of successive generations. Society, as a result, must decide whether it wants its textbooks to be shaped by pressure groups or by scholars seeking to supply the most accurate information available. Too often, society has yielded to the pressure groups.

After the Civil War, it was natural, perhaps, that both the North and the South should try to dictate their own versions of the history of the conflict and see to it that textbooks supported their views. Veterans on each side still contended for the regional loyalties they carried into battle, and they were willing to bring pressure on publishers and authors.

The resistance they met from the publishing houses was far less spirited than that they had met on the battlefield. Some publishers surrendered to the demands of the veterans without firing a shot. In 1867, just two years after the war, E. J. Hale and Son of New York advertised: "Books prepared for southern schools, by southern authors, and therefore free from matter offensive to southern people."

Most publishers, however, attempted to print histories that would sell both in the North and the South. More often than not, they encountered sales resistance in each of the regions. In 1892, the United Confederate Veterans ordered its new historical committee to denounce unsatisfactory books and recommend acceptable ones for use in the South's public and private schools. The committee, under the leadership of General Stephen Lee of Mississippi, soon announced that almost every northern-published history was unfair to the Confederacy. What should Southern pupils read? The veterans committee suggested *The Southern Side of the Prison Question; A Confederate View of the Treatment of Prisoners;* and histories by Jefferson Davis, Alexander H. Stephens and other Confederate leaders.

The historical committee established subcommittees in each state and directed them to screen every history text in use in the schools. Under pressure from a subcommittee, the state board of education in Virginia dropped *A Brief History of the United States* and added textbooks by such writers as J. William Jones, a leader of the United Confederate Veterans. Other subcommittees rallied the support of the United Sons of Confederate Veterans and the United Daughters of the Confederacy and brought textbooks under fire in both Carolinas, Georgia, Florida, Texas, Alabama and Mississippi.

In the North, the Grand Army Record urged Union veterans to "aid in dashing down the cup of moral poison that our school histories are holding to your youth." A committee of the Grand Army of the Republic charged in 1897 that no book then in use "merits the unqualified endorsement of this organization."

One text, *Leading Facts of American History* by D. H. Montgomery, was a frequent target of GAR criticism. When a distinguished historian, Professor Albert Bushnell Hart of Harvard, defended the book, the *Grand Army Record* led a counterattack: "If he [Hart] had been the paid attorney of Montgomery and his publishers in a professional way, he would have defended Montgomery in precisely the way that he has elected to defend him." The name of every Massachusetts town using Montgomery's book in its schools was listed by the *Grand Army Record* in a "Roll of Dishonor."

A Brief History of the United States, a book designed for national distribution, irritated Northerners as well as Southerners. A textbook committee of the New York Grand Army attacked the book because the flag was mentioned only once and the words "traitor," "treason," and "patriotism" not at all.

Neither the North nor the South, however, would settle for the simple deletion or addition of words. The publishing firms reconciled themselves to the situation and followed the lead of the firm which, in 1897, had offered tailor-made histories. They began publishing regional textbooks, one version for the South and another for the North, and, as a result, fogged the minds of students for more than two generations.

The aftermath of World War I produced a new rash of textbook criticism. Those who grew up in later generations may be surprised to learn how much of it was aimed at a wartime ally, Great Britain.

In his series of articles for the Hearst newspapers, Charles Grant Miller warned parents against "Anglicized" histories. "It makes a mighty difference," he said, "whether America continues to quick-step to 'Yankee Doodle' or takes to marking time to 'God Save the King.'" Using a system of textbook criticism another Hearst writer was to employ for the Los Angeles *Herald-Examiner* in 1961 and 1962, Miller counted lines in the textbooks and was outraged when an historical figure he disliked received more attention than one he admired.

Few books escaped the wrath of Miller, who frequently enraged eminent historians by quoting them out of context to support his claims of British subversion. Ironically, however, *A Brief History of the United States,* an updated version of the book that had troubled the Civil War veterans, found a strong admirer in Miller. He announced that the book spoke "always from the American viewpoint, with American interests and sympathies at heart."

While the Hearst newspapers failed to impress the historians with the anti-textbook articles, they succeeded in launching a wave of censorship. In New York, Mayor Hylan appointed David Hirshfield, the city's commissioner of accounts, to carry out a textbook investigation. According to the New York *Times* and the *Tribune,* Hirschfield hired a historian, Joseph Devlin, to report on unpatriotic texts, but then abandoned Devlin's report when it failed to blast the books. Hirshfield next turned to a man he knew would do the job he wanted – Charles Grant Miller.

In 1922, the American Legion commissioned the writing of a textbook in American history which would "preach on every page a vivid love of America." The Veterans of Foreign Wars established its National Americanization Committee and directed it to work toward the "elimination of un-American textbooks." By the late 1920s, the VFW announced that it had "eliminated all of the objectionable features" in American histories and was turning its attention to modern European volumes.

The VFW may have been pleased with the American histories, but William Hart Thompson, the mayor of Chicago, was not. In 1927 and 1928, "Big Bill the Builder" unleashed a scathing series of attacks on history texts, particularly those that treated the Revolutionary War. In his campaign for a third term as mayor, Thompson charged that the King of England himself had persuaded Chicago's superintendent of schools to remove George Washington's picture from the books.

German- and Irish-Americans cast huge votes in Chicago, and Thompson, who was frequently called "Kaiser Bill" by his opponents, found it politically helpful to oppose the British. "Chicago," Thompson once explained, "is the sixth largest German city in the world." Thompson succeeded in having the Chicago superintendent of schools fired on charges of insubordination and pro-British sympathies. But the mayor's attacks on school texts continued. He told his electorate that American histories "bristle with fulsome laudation of British democracy, British ideas, British institutions and British achievements, those of America being made to appear as poor imitations."

The attacks on the textbooks in the twenties got results. The Oregon Legislature instructed educators to select no book "which speaks slightingly of the founders of the Republic, or the men who preserved the union. . . ." Legislators in Wisconsin and Oklahoma took similar action, and censorship bills came close to passing in New York and New Jersey. Textbook investigations were ordered in Pennsylvania and in many cities and towns across the nation.

In 1936, looking back on the post–World War I attacks on the way the history of the American Revolution was being taught, Howard K. Beale brought out his book *Are American Teachers Free?* On the question of how Americans gained their independence, Beale decided, teachers and historians could have escaped the attacks of the twenties only by distorting history. He said the critics wanted to deny schoolchildren the right to learn that "British colonists in America were allowed more freedom than any other colonists in the world, that they had more voice in their own government than did the Englishmen in England, and that it was only because they had so much freedom that they had been able to develop the strength and initiative to win independence."

Many of the textbook censors, Beale showed in his well-documented book, were successful in getting authors and publishers to conform to their prejudices. Phrases such as "the colonies were not desperately oppressed" were removed from Albert Bushnell Hart's *School History of the United States.* And passages saying that many colonists doubted the wisdom of separating from Britain were struck from David S. Muzzey's *American History* and other popular texts. These concessions, added to those won by the Civil War veterans, meant that students were now getting incomplete accounts of two of the most important chapters in American history.

Although charges of pro-British sentiment bulked large in the controversies of the twenties, groups other than the Hearst newspapers and individuals other than Mayor Thompson had their causes to advance. The multiplicity of the groups and causes, and the many and often inconsistent angles of attack, may well seem bewildering. For one, the Ku Klux Klan raised its voice.

"It is notorious," said the Klan, "that our public school system, which is the strongest bulwark of Americanism, is being attacked from within and without by papists and anti-Christian Jews of the Bolshevik Socialist stripe."

The Klan objected in particular to books which credited Columbus, instead of Leif Ericson, with the discovery of America. In the same era, the Knights of Columbus announced that they wanted history books to "make it plain that the lessons taught by the life of Columbus were as dear to the Catholic citizen as were those inspired and inculcated by the ideals of George Washington."

The anti-evolutionists also railed against textbooks. To win sales in Texas and other anti-Darwinian hotbeds, some publishing houses struck references to evolution from their volumes. Henry Holt and Company removed chapters on the evolution of man from Moon's *Biology for Beginners* and the Macmillan Company deleted the word "evolution" from *Healthful Living* by Jesse F. Williams.

A good example of the difficulties a writer faced in meeting contradictory charges from groups with different interests was David Muzzey and his *American History*. The Daughters of the American Revolution said Muzzey did not place enough emphasis on military history to make good soldiers out of children. But the National Council for the Prevention of War said the histories should stress the peace-loving qualities of America's heroes. At the same time, the American School Citizenship League and the National Education Association felt histories should give attention to international as well as American heroes and teach history from the world point of view.

Organized labor was interested in seeing that the cause of labor was given favorable treatment in the school texts. In 1929, the Committee on Education of the American Federation of Labor announced that it had completed a survey of social science textbooks: "The majority of publishers were cooperative, realizing that such a review as the Federation has undertaken, was a service to them as well as to the schools. A number of publishers have safeguarded their books by asking the Federation to read manuscripts so that they could benefit by criticism in advance of publication."

Ironically, at the very time the AFL was claiming success for its screening program, the Federal Trade Commission was exposing the textbook-doctoring campaign of the public utilities industry. The utilities officials did not court front-page headlines as Mayor Thompson had done in Chicago. They preferred to operate in private conferences with school superintendents and presidents of publishing houses. As a result, the nation was shocked by the disclosures made by the Federal Trade Commission over a three-year period beginning in 1928. FTC investigators learned that the National Electric Light Association, the American Gas Association, the American Railway Association and many of their member corporations had attempted – and often succeeded – in placing the utilities' own interpretation of history before the nation's children.

Utilities tycoon Samuel Insull, worried by what he

thought was a trend toward municipal ownership of utilities, established a censorship pattern for the utilities companies in 1919. His first step was to create the Illinois Public Welfare and Public Utility Educational Service to "make the public better acquainted with the fundamental economic facts of the public utility industry." Soon after it was organized, the committee examined civics and economics texts in use in the Illinois schools. It labeled fourteen of the books "bad" from the point of view of the utilities; one "very bad," and another "unfair."

News of the work of the Illinois committee spread among utilities officials and led to similar textbook studies in Missouri, New York, Pennsylvania, New Jersey, North and South Carolina, Ohio, Texas, Iowa, Wisconsin, Colorado, Michigan, Washington and California. By 1925, the National Electric Light Association could tell its members that "some of the state bureaus have accomplished a very important task in having removed from school textbooks any unfair, biased, incorrect and misleading statements concerning public utilities." In the same year, the director of the utility information committee in Iowa reported that he had called the "obnoxious books" to the attention of school officials and, as a result, the matter "was pretty well in hand."

The utilities wanted to do more than censor existing books. They wanted new books specially written for the nation's classrooms. In 1925 one of Samuel Insull's employes wrote another utilities official that he was making progress in negotiations with publishing houses. "We have had nothing so far but encouragement in handling the matter through publishers," F. R. Jenkins wrote. "I feel that we have made a good start in getting the largest school book publishing house . . . with us which will be a tremendous leverage on any other house should opposition occur, which I doubt." According to testimony before the Federal Trade Commission, utilities officials reached an agreement with the John C. Winston Company of Philadelphia allowing them to check over new textbooks dealing with public utilities.

While waiting for new textbooks to appear, the utilities financed promotional pamphlets and had them distributed to the public schools. The schools in Ohio alone were inundated with 136,000 copies of one booklet, *Aladdins of Industry*.

During the propaganda drive, some utilities officials worried that their activities would be exposed. In a letter to another official, the manager of the St. Joseph Gas Company in Missouri warned that "great care must be used to avoid going too far since if the public were to get the idea that textbooks were being used as propaganda for the public utility companies the reaction would be worse than the original misinformation."

The manager's worst fears were realized when the Federal Trade Commission investigation began. The public outcry proved sufficient to discourage textbook attacks from most quarters for several years. Only a few venturesome organizations – the Woman's Christian Temperance Union and the Florida Chamber of Commerce – were willing to challenge the textbooks. In gathering information for his *Are American Teachers Free?*, Howard Beale talked to one publisher who had just issued a new text on social hygiene. Beale said the publisher told him the book "was written to avoid raising any more objection from the liquor people than necessary, and yet, at the same time, to please the

WCTU forces." The Florida Chamber of Commerce complained in the early thirties because a geography text contained more pictures of California than of Florida.

When textbook criticism erupted again on a wide scale in 1939, it was almost as if the ten years' respite had been used by the critics in gaining momentum for the new assault. In a series of attacks that extended until the outbreak of World War II, the foes of the textbooks used both the eagle-screaming tactics of Chicago's Mayor Thompson and the efficient, behind-the-scenes methods of the utility interests. Outraged citizens tossed an armful of books in the school furnace in Bradner, Ohio, and burned a fiery cross in front of the home of the school board president. The National Association of Manufacturers was less violent and more methodical. It financed a textbook study that resulted in lengthy charges against many books. Despite the differences in approach, however, the attacks that began in 1939 had one common target – they focused on a mild-mannered Columbia University professor and his series of social science texts.

The Columbia professor of education, Dr. Harold Rugg, began planning for his series of books in 1920. Operating on borrowed money, he hired two research assistants and began producing experimental books for use in "pilot" schools. He used the money he received for the experimental books to boost his research team to sixteen assistants and started devising a complete social science program for the schools. Rugg was determined to spare neither time nor expense. As he saw it, his books would, for the first time, make the complex problems of history, government and society in general come alive for the child. He particularly wanted his texts to deal with controversial issues. "To keep issues out of the school . . . is to keep thought out of it," Dr. Rugg said. "It is to keep life out of it."

Finally, in 1930, Rugg issued his first series of commercial texts – six 600-page volumes for the junior high school. They won immediate acclaim from educators, and schools throughout the nation began adopting them. Rugg used his royalties to produce still more texts, and by 1939 he had published two more junior high school volumes and eight for the elementary grades. His combined output was selling then at the rate of nearly 300,000 a year and Rugg was being recognized as a leading educator.

It had taken Rugg twenty years to achieve success, but his attackers were to relieve him of it in less than a sixth of that time. The first major attack came in the summer of 1939 when the Advertising Federation of America urged its sixty affiliated agencies to campaign against books which placed the advertising industry in an unfavorable light. With the appeal went a pamphlet attacking one of Rugg's volumes, *An Introduction to the Problems of American Culture*. The book, which was in use in 4200 school systems containing nearly half of the nation's schoolchildren, said that "it would be impossible to carry on our economic life today without advertising." The advertising federation had no objection to that statement, but the book went further: "We must ask ourselves if all the advertising today is wise and necessary." Rugg's book then accused the advertising industry of misrepresenting goods, of improper use of testimonials and of encouraging people to buy to the point of extravagance. It also praised the advertising federation for taking steps to eliminate objectionable advertising practices. But the Federation regretted that Rugg's "discussion of our work is much too brief, compared with the opposing text."

Bertie C. Forbes, long-time columnist for the Hearst newspapers and publisher of *Forbes Magazine,* assailed the Rugg books from his position on the board of education in Englewood, New Jersey. He was joined by Merwin K. Hart, the president of the New York State Economic Council, who was to receive publicity in the fifties as an anti-Semite and in the sixties as a leader in New York circles of the John Birch Society.

"Are Rugg books in your schools?" a Hart newsletter asked in April, 1940. "We recommend that our members and readers in all localities ascertain whether these Rugg social science texts are in use in their schools. And if you let us know what you find we will try to make constructive suggestions."

The early attacks on Rugg were glancing blows, however, compared to the assaults which were to come. In its September, 1940, issue, the *American Legion Magazine* struck at Rugg and several other textbook authors in an article, "Treason in the Textbooks," by O. K. Armstrong of Springfield, Missouri. An accompanying cartoon showed a school teacher leering at frightened pupils and dripping slime from his hands upon four books labeled "Constitution," "Religion," "U. S. Heroes," and "U. S. History." The caption read: "The 'Frontier Thinkers' are trying to sell our youth the idea that the American Way of Life has failed."

Another attack came from the National Association of Manufacturers, which hired Dr. Ralph West Robey, an assistant professor of banking at Columbia University, to make a study of American textbooks. Robey soon contended that American texts, particularly those by Rugg, were laced with anti-business sentiment and economic-determinist and socialistic theories. In reporting the results of Robey's study, *Time* called the nation's schoolbooks "New Dealish," but indicated it did not consider Robey to be an impartial critic. Robey, said the magazine, was a "high Tory."

Shortly before his books were brought under organized attack, Rugg completed a 20,000-mile tour of the United States. He talked to dozens of educators in every part of the country to gather material for a new series of texts. Nowhere, he later recalled, did he hear a "whisper" of opposition to his books. A year and a half later, he was on another tour of the country, attending public hearings again and again to defend himself and his books. Where Rugg had found not even a whisper of criticism, he now found almost a continuous shout. At a Georgia Board of Education hearing, a state police captain pointed at Rugg and yelled: "There sits the ringmaster of the fifth columnists in America, financed by the Russian government."

"I am not a Communist," Rugg said repeatedly at the hearings. "I have never been a Communist. I have never been a member of or affiliated with the Communist party, directly or indirectly in any way whatsoever. I am not a Socialist. I have never been a Socialist. I have never been a member of or affiliated with the Socialist party. Nor have I taken part in the work of that party." When Rugg recounted his experiences in his book *That Men May Understand,* he recalled that the "most astounding fact" revealed in the hearings was that few of his accusers had read the books. Rugg said:

"Person after person started out with the same phrase: 'I haven't read the books, but . . .'

" 'I haven't read the books, but – I have heard of the author and no good about him.'

" 'I haven't read the books, but – he's from Columbia and that's enough.' . . . 'I hear that chapel isn't required any more in the universities like Columbia.'

" 'I haven't read the books, but – my brother says the schools and colleges are filled with Communists.' "

Many of Rugg's critics based their opposition to him on grounds that he was a "Deweyite," an apostle of the educational philosopher John Dewey. And the anti-Rugg forces quoted much more frequently from one book Rugg had written for adults (*The Great Technology*) than from the many volumes he had published for children. In *The Great Technology,* Rugg told educators:

> Every form of government on earth today must be regarded frankly as an experiment, tentative and to be changed as new social and economic conditions develop. The trend has revealed scores of experiments, and a great variety of forms and methods of collective thinking. The danger is that the young national in each of the sixty countries will grow up with the conviction that the form peculiar to his country is of proven superiority, rather than that it is one of many experiments which can be greatly improved by the substitution of many foreign experiences. . . .

Rugg urged his attackers to judge *The Great Technology* "in the light of the distressing conditions existing in late 1932 and early 1933, the very moment when it was being written." He said his opponents "forget that they themselves accepted, even welcomed, the acts of the welfare government as it rescued them from the brink of collapse on which they tottered on March 4, 1933 – the very acts which they now so violently condemn."

But Rugg's appeals did little to change the course of the

opposition to him. As one school district banned his books, another followed in chain reaction. Only in a few communities, like Englewood, New Jersey, did citizens' groups succeed in retaining the Rugg textbooks in the schools.

Rugg's books eventually disappeared from all classrooms, but the textbook critics have not forgotten them. In 1958 the *American Legion Magazine* said, "Rugg textbooks are no longer used in our schools, but the ideas that they planted are like the hardy germs of the new 'golden staphylococcus' – they're highly resistant to all known antibodies." And in Meriden, Connecticut, in 1961, Edward Casey and Fred Dobson prefaced their attacks on textbooks by announcing almost prayerfully: "Fortunate is the fact that the public schools in Meriden are not using the Rugg social science texts."

Textbook critics not only continue to attack the defunct Rugg series, but they utilize information gathered in the Rugg controversy to launch new campaigns against new books. More important, censors can draw from the Rugg controversy a lesson that textbook publishers cannot fail to ignore: organized attacks on texts can prove highly successful. In 1938, the sales of Rugg's high-school and elementary texts had totaled 289,000 copies. Six years later, they had dwindled ninety per cent to 21,000 copies.

3

Toward the Present

ONCE, an aspiring book-banner had to read a text to sound authoritative when criticizing it. That bit of drudgery was banished in 1949, however, when Lucille Cardin Crain began using a quarterly newsletter to cite passages and page numbers from books which might "subvert" the school child. With the *Educational Reviewer* in hand, almost anyone could convince a school board that he had made a detailed study of instructional material.

In addition to her efficiency, Mrs. Crain brought charm into the fight against textbooks. A writer for *McCall's* magazine, interviewing her in 1951 when she was fifty, departed with a compelling description for his readers. "She does possess the most attractive figure in the anti-school movement," Arthur D. Morse wrote. "She . . . has cool blue eyes, a cameo face and a fondness for using rather fancy words."

Mrs. Crain also had a fondness for assailing textbooks. In the first issue of the *Educational Reviewer,* she engaged Edna Lonigan of New York to appraise *American Government,* a high-school text by Frank Abbott Magruder. Miss

Lonigan professed to be appalled at the book, which, in various editions, had been in use for thirty-eight years. As she saw it, Magruder's view of democracy led "straight from Rousseau, through Marx, to totalitarianism." To document her charges, she quoted a passage to show that Magruder was advocating collectivism: "By Democracy we mean that form of government in which the sovereign power is in the hands of the people collectively." The quote was correct insofar as it went, but she put a period where Magruder had placed a comma. What Magruder actually said was: "By democracy we mean that form of government in which the sovereign power is in the hands of the people collectively, and is expressed by them either directly or indirectly through elected representatives."

The *Reviewer* also accused Magruder of saying that "the United States and the Soviet Union are equals fighting for 'world leadership.'" Magruder really said that "the United States and the Soviet Union, the most powerful of the allies in the Second World War, now find themselves as the only two powerful contenders for world leadership."

The *Reviewer* further charged that he stated: "Italy and Germany were dictatorships but not the Soviet Union." Again, Magruder had put it differently: "Russia is leader of the dictatorial nations, most of which are communistic."

The *Reviewer* convinced itself that the book was undermining the free enterprise system. It also convinced a good many others, including radio commentator Fulton Lewis, Jr. A few months after the *Reviewer's* analysis, Lewis used portions of it on a coast-to-coast broadcast and added a comment of his own: "And that's the book that has been in use in high schools all over the nation, possibly by your youngster."

Mrs. Crain, who held no college degrees, could count her first venture into book reviewing a success. Outraged parents brought the text under attack in Englewood, New Jersey; Port Washington, Long Island; Washington, D.C., and many other parts of the nation. Boards of Education banned it outright in Richland, Washington; Houston, Texas; Little Rock, Arkansas; Lafayette, Indiana; and throughout the state of Georgia.

The Atlanta *Constitution* protested the school board's action in Georgia, observing that "Governor Talmadge was taught from the book, as were most of the men and women in public life in Georgia, and we defy the board to prove it has made subversives, socialists, or radicals of them." Mrs. Julius Y. Talmadge, a member of the Georgia board and a former national regent of the DAR, replied that the volume contained "controversial material," and issues of a controversial nature, she said, had no place in a Georgia classroom. Neither Mrs. Talmadge nor her colleagues of the board seemed concerned, however, over how the Magruder text might affect children in other states. They offered to sell 30,000 copies to school systems outside Georgia.

Dr. Magruder, a University of Washington professor who used his book royalties to finance a summer camp for victims of polio, died just as the attacks against him were commencing. But small groups of school teachers fighting in his behalf, insisted that his text be given fair hearings. In Council Bluffs, Iowa, and Jackson, Michigan, educators reexamined the book and prepared a lengthy defense of it — a step that ended pressure for its removal. School board members in Florida; New Haven, Connecticut; and Trumbull County in Ohio, on reading the book, found it satisfactory for school use. Eventually, Little Rock, Houston and the state of Georgia reinstated the volume, though only after the publisher, Allyn and Bacon, agreed to make some revisions and deletions. Even Mrs. Talmadge, who had led the anti-Magruder forces in Georgia, dropped her opposition upon assurances that the publisher would delete some of its references to the United Nations.

While school boards around the nation were debating the book, Mrs. Crain and her staff were busily examining other texts. Many of them, including the *American Way of Life* by Harry E. Barnes and *Modern Economics* by James F. Corbitt and Minna Colvin, sorely displeased the *Reviewer*. As in the case of the attack on Magruder, the criticism fell on a responsive audience. "Every school trustee in this country and every school administrator ought to subscribe to the *Educational Reviewer*," the Chicago Sunday *Tribune* exhorted in January, 1950. "Most of them would do so, we are sure, if they knew of the existence of this uniquely valuable publication."

The *Educational Reviewer* might have continued screening textbooks indefinitely if the activities of its sponsor, the Conference of American Small Business Organizations, had not come under scrutiny by the House Committee on Lobbying Activities. Although Mrs. Crain had announced in every issue that her newsletter was being sponsored by CASBO, her readers either did not know or did not care that CASBO was an active lobbying organization. The House committee took a different view. In a report to Congress it said: "The review of textbooks by self-appointed experts, especially when undertaken under the aegis of an organization having a distinctive legislative axe to grind, smacks too much of the book burning orgies of Nuremberg to be accepted by thoughtful Americans without foreboding and alarm. It suggests, too, that the reviewers profoundly distrust the integrity, good faith, and plain common sense of school boards and teachers of the country." The congressional committtee added that it was convinced that the long-term objective of the *Educational Reviewer* "is nothing less than the establishment of [its own] philosophy as the standard educational orthodoxy in the schools of the nation."

After the committee report appeared in 1951, two magazines, *McCall's* and *Commentary,* published articles showing how Mrs. Crain and her *Reviewer* had generated many book controversies which, on their surface, appeared to have resulted from spontaneous outbursts by parents. Within three years, the *Reviewer* folded. But educators were to hear from Mrs. Crain again in 1958 when she once more lent her talents to textbook criticism, this time as chief of the reviewing operation of America's Future, Inc., an organization which will be discussed in detail in a later chapter of this book.

Mrs. Crain's *Reviewer* operated in a tense period of American history. Within the four-year life span of her publication, Russia became increasingly aggressive; Communist armies forced Chiang Kai-shek from the Chinese mainland and engaged the United Nations in war in Korea; in the United States, newspapers brimmed with accounts of Communist espionage activities and charges — by Senator Joseph McCarthy and others — that Reds had penetrated deep into government. Given this atmosphere of strain and suspicion, it was not unnatural that the *Reviewer* and other publications and organizations should lay a foundation for attacks on textbooks that would survive until the nineteen-sixties. Mrs. Crain's contribution to present day campaigns against books was the mass reviewing technique. Other organizations and publications contributed "blacklists" of books and authors.

One group, which in the early stages of the Cold War compiled data still figuring in textbook controversies, was the Sons of the American Revolution. Enthusiastic after having won a legislative investigation of instructional materials in California, the SAR began agitating in 1949 for an inquiry on a national scale. To aid their appeal to Congress, they prepared a fifty-four-page booklet, *A Bill of Grievances,* which warned of "interstate traffic in propaganda textbooks and teaching materials."

"Our schools are being converted into agencies for the dissemination of radical propaganda, most of which originates in Communist front organizations and other pressure groups," the Sons declared in their *Bill.* "Gullible or indoctrinated 'liberals' supporting these organizations appear to be responsible for this condition."

In building their case, the Sons exhumed ten-year-old charges against the Rugg social science books and charged that another group of texts (Building America) "contained material originating from one hundred and thirteen fronts." No other textbooks were cited in the *Bill,* but the Sons listed the names of hundreds of writers and scholars, who, in the thirties, had signed petitions welcoming Russian missions to the United States or urging, in 1939, "closer cooperation" with Soviet Russia. Entwined in the appeal for a textbook investigation was an attack on the Supreme Court and the National Education Association.

In 1962, despite the fact that much of its information was then twenty-three years old, the *Bill* was still highly regarded by textbook censors as a "basic research" document; and organizations — the Daughters of the American Revolution, for one — listed it among literature available to their members.

One of the key exhibits the Sons included with their *Bill* was a pamphlet, *Red-ucators at Harvard,* which was published by the National Council for American Education. The name of this organization was similar enough to the names of the National Education Association and the American Council on Education to confuse many people. All similarity among the three organizations ended with their corporate titles, however. The NEA and the American Council actively promote the cause of public education. The National Council for American Education was organized by a balding chronic agitator, Allen A. Zoll, who attacked not only textbooks but the entire American educational system.

"Doctor" Zoll, as Frederick Woltman was to point out in a story for the New York *World-Telegram,* had been an almost professional anti-Semite before becoming an "educator." In 1939, he appeared at a Senate hearing to oppose the nomination of Felix Frankfurter as a justice of the United States Supreme Court. He disliked Frankfurter's record, for one thing; and, for another, he abhorred his religion. "So far as I am concerned," Senator Borah told Zoll, "I do not propose to listen to an argument against a man because of his religion. You are raising the same question that is drenching Europe in blood."

At the time of his appearance before the Senate committee, Zoll was heading American Patriots, Inc., a group included by the Attorney General on a 1947 list of "totalitarian, fascist, communist or subversive" organizations. After abandoning American Patriots and before forming his education council, Zoll worked as a salesman for Merwin K. Hart, who had been active in the campaign against the Rugg social science series in the early forties.

Combining his selling experience with his flair for organization, Zoll succeeded in lining up an imposing list of personages for his board of governors when he opened his education office in 1948. But several of the board members – including boxer Gene Tunney and General Jonathan Wainwright – handed in their resignations after Zoll's past activities were exposed in the *World-Telegram*.

Zoll's organization was crippled, but not put out of business entirely, by the publicity which surrounded the Tunney and Wainwright resignations. Zoll continued mailing anti–school-text propaganda and making speeches around the country to organizations like the Minute Women of the U.S.A., Inc. whose founder and national chairman, Suzanne Silvercruys Stevenson, was fond of warning that "true American textbooks" were being replaced with new and dangerous ones. Often on his lecture tours Zoll was introduced as "Doctor," a title he received from a diploma mill operated by a man who had served a prison sentence for fraud.

Assisting Zoll in his attacks on texts was Verne Kaub, a writer for an anti-Jewish publication, the *Individualist*. Kaub, according to Arthur Morse's article in *McCall's,* was not without his problems in trying to bring textbooks under suspicion. Morse said Zoll told him: "Once we had to have a book reviewed eight times before we got a good analysis."

Zoll's pamphlets denouncing progressive education and tax-supported schools figured in a bitter school fight in Pasadena, California, an almost classical education battle which led to the ousting of a school superintendent. The textbook reviews distributed by Kaub turned up during controversies in Englewood, New Jersey, and in Tennessee, where the outcry led to the creation of a legislative investigation commission. But after the investigators had been at work for two weeks, the Nashville *Tennessean* observed that "the textbook probe has been a fizzle from the very beginning . . . the committee has not received a single complaint citing specific passages in Tennessee texts as subversive."

Although the National Council for American Education squeaked past its first brush with publicity, it, like Mrs. Crain's *Reviewer,* lost its effectiveness after sustained exposure in newspapers and magazines. Zoll and Kaub dropped from public view for a few years only to return to the fight against "subversion" in the sixties. Kaub's new targets were "Red" clergymen, and he attacked them through an organization he called the American Council of Christian Laymen. After an abortive effort to form the Federation of Conservatives, Zoll served on the staff of the Rev. Billy James Hargis and his Christian Crusade for a few months in 1961. And Hargis, a self-styled fighter of Communism, proudly announced that he had acquired Zoll's "priceless" files. These files, said Hargis, included "the names of thousands of clergymen and educators who have chosen to affiliate with communist front organizations over the years."

Another organization attacking textbooks in the early years of the Cold War was the Guardians of American Education. Organized in 1940, the Guardians fought to ban books written by Harold Rugg and other "Frontier Thinkers." The organization became inactive soon after it was founded, but was revived in 1952 under the leadership of Augustin G. Rudd, whose book *Bending the Twig* is still quoted by textbook censors. In one of their brochures, the Guardians declared that "we are firmly convinced that this republic will not endure if *so many of our schools and colleges* continue to spawn Marxists, whether they be collectivists, Socialists or Communists."

Under Rudd's leadership, the Guardians specialized in mailing out reprints of articles from the *American Legion Magazine:* "Your Child is Their Target," by Irene Corbally Kuhn; "Our Academic Hucksters," by E. Merrill Root. By publishing the Kuhn article, which was being distributed prior to publication date by the Guardians, the Legion's magazine drew criticism from within the Legion's own ranks. "This Irene Kuhn," said Legion Post 173 in Dearborn, Michigan, "states that . . . we use Communist-influenced textbooks by 'subversive' teachers, and that our progressive education is only teaching our students to have no respect for parents or law and order, and that our schools are merely just a mass of confusion. Then in the next breath she states that we are regimenting our children after the pattern of Adolph Hitler's youth movement. . . . In one sentence, we give our students too much freedom with no control and in the next paragraph we don't give them any freedom!"

Since the early days of the Cold War, textbook crises have come in an almost unbroken stream, each controversy providing fuel for another. In most instances only the names of the towns and the censors are different. The charges are essentially the same: the texts are blamed for what a censor dislikes about the world in which he lives.

While Lucille Cardin Crain and Allen Zoll were campaigning against textbooks on a national scale, the citizens of

Scarsdale, New York, were feuding among themselves over what children should and should not read. By the sixties, the Scarsdale case had been at rest for nearly a decade, but it continued to fascinate students of academic freedom, perhaps because it demonstrated clearly that textbook controversy can develop anywhere. Scarsdale was, indeed, an unlikely spot to look for opposition to the free enterprise system. The chances were great in the late forties, when the censorship attempts began, that anyone you stopped on a Scarsdale street would be both prosperous and a Republican. Almost any resident could tell you that little Westchester County, which embraces Scarsdale, supplied New York with some of its top executives and had a greater representation in *Who's Who* in proportion to its population than any other county in the nation.

Yet the school board, which was thoroughly representative of Scarsdale's citizenry, was brought under suspicion by a tiny segment of the community because of the books it was permitting the children to use. The opening round of the two-year fight occurred when a "Committee of Ten" objected because books by Howard Fast, Anna Louise Strong, Louis Untermeyer and Shirley Graham were on the shelves of the school libraries.

"I don't care what a man's politics or his religion are if he writes a good book," one board member, a lawyer, told the censors. Other Scarsdale residents responded by rushing to buy copies of novels by Howard Fast, a writer who had not denied a Communist party affiliation. Within weeks, there were waiting lists for Fast's works at public libraries and bookstores in the area. Later, when the local American Legion post declared itself in favor of banning books by "leftist authors," Scarsdale was forced to take the attacks seriously.

Soon, the town was gripped in controversy, and dozens of Scarsdale's most active citizens (including Charles E. Wilson, president of General Electric, and Harry E. Humphreys, Jr., president of United States Rubber) signed a public statement in an attempt to head off the book-banning efforts. "We do not minimize the dangers of Communist and fascist indoctrination, but we want to meet these dangers in the American way," they said. "A state that fears to permit the expression of views alternative to those held by the majority is a state that does not trust itself. . . . Any sensible person would agree that there are risks involved in allowing young persons relatively free access to a wide range of reading material. Of course, there are risks. But we believe there are greater risks in any alternative procedure. Surely we have not, as a people, lost the courage to take the risks that are necessary for the preservation of freedom."

While the statement of principle impressed a good many persons, it did not succeed in halting the efforts of the small group which insisted on purging the bookshelves. The attack on books was broadened, in fact, to include several textbooks in addition to the library volumes. But after winning an overwhelming endorsement in a town meeting and enduring two years of controversy, the school board wearily voted to hear no more argument about books.

Agitation against "subversive" texts in Scarsdale and other areas of New York led the state to establish a Special Regents Commission in 1952 to investigate complaints against instructional materials. During the first twenty months of its existence the commission did not receive a single complaint – a development which led the New York

Times to say that the charges against the texts "must indeed have been so wild that their originators did not think that they could stand the light of a fair hearing."

Alabama, in trying to please the agitators there, passed a law in 1953 which made many publishers fearful of even attempting to sell a text in the state. The statute required them to preface every book distributed in Alabama with a statement as to whether any authors cited in the book for parallel reading had ever advocated Communism, Marxist Socialism or been a member of a Communist front organization. Twenty-five publishers, in a rare display of concerted action against textbook critics, contested the act in the courts. They said the statement required by the Alabama law could open them to countless lawsuits from authors. Statisticians at the Alabama Polytechnic Institute estimated that 28,000,000 names, including duplications, would have to be investigated before the publishers could comply with the act. Eventually the courts ruled that the statute violated the due process clause of the Fourteenth Amendment.

Modern textbooks had been flailed again and again by the mid-fifties, so perhaps it was natural that Mrs. Ada White, a member of the Indiana State Textbook Commission, should dig far into the past to unearth a new villian. Robin Hood and his "merry men," she told her startled colleagues on the commission, were following the "straight communist line" while dashing through Sherwood Forest in the twelfth century. And, she added, all books containing the Robin Hood story and its "rob the rich to give the poor" philosophy should be banned forthwith from the Indiana schools. But, for once, the foes of book-banning had all the support they could possibly want. Perhaps Robin Hood should henceforth be called "Robin Hoodski," chuckled the Rock Hill, South Carolina *Herald*. In England, even the Sheriff of Nottingham, successor to the storied foe of the merry bandits of Sherwood Forest, hastened to Robin's defense.

In California in 1957 a legislator hunted bigger game than Robin Hood. State Senator Hugh P. Donnally introduced a bill to prohibit the use of schoolbooks judged at variance with "morality, truth, justice or patriotism." Donnally's colleagues in the legislature, however, wondering just who would pass on all those virtues, killed the bill in committee. The Senate action came in face of protests from the California League of Christian Parents, whose president condemned literature from the United Nations and UNESCO as "Godless, atheistic and un-American."

Other Californians were also taking a dim view of school texts in 1957. The Santa Ana *Register* assailed a college chemistry book on the ground that it was subtly campaigning for fluoridation. And in Kern County a grand jury recommended the removal of a number of elementary and high school books, charging that several were "socialistic." One volume that would have disappeared from the library shelves had the grand jury had its way was *A Foreign Policy for Americans* by the late Senator Robert Taft. The jurors said Taft, the leader of American conservatives in his generation, gave a "one-sided view of the United Nations."

Despite the flurry of controversy in California, the long chain of anti-textbook campaigns sparked by Cold War tensions was beginning to flag in 1957. The lull was to be a short one, however. The Russians fanned tensions anew by firing a Sputnik into orbit; and a small-college professor played on popular unrest with a book that ushered in the present wave of censorship.

4

E. Merrill Root

IN A LITTLE red farmhouse, just off a dirt road in the scraggy hills of northwest Rhode Island, lives a mild-mannered poet, a retired college English professor. More than two years away from the classroom now, he enjoys devoting more time to poetry and the outdoor life – fishing, boating, walking in the woodlands and target shooting ("I like guns and have a lot of them, but I don't hunt because I can't stand to kill anything"). But what absorbs him most is writing and talking about "collectivists" monopolizing the nation's education system, "brainwashing" students into accepting anti-American ideas.

A short, portly man, softspoken and gracious, sensitive to criticism, E. Merrill Root appears the very opposite of the raucous image that springs from some of his virulent writings about "subversion" in education. He looks more the part of the poet and retired professor than the indignant patriot and hunter of subversion. He is a good listener. He talks candidly about his beliefs. However much one might disagree with what he says, it is apparent he believes he is right and the great majority of the nation's educators wrong. He believes that most historians and college professors, most textbook authors and publishers, and a high percentage of public-school teachers and administrators, some wittingly and others unwittingly, are distorting history, defaming the American heritage, turning the country into a collectivist and perhaps Communist state. And he believes that he somehow has providential guidance in his efforts to turn the tide.

Root was a little-known English professor in a small Quaker college in Indiana in the early 1950s when he began his hunt for Communists and Marxist propaganda in the education system. Today he wields more influence than any other man in the attempts of pressure groups to rewrite American textbooks. His supporters call him a "patriot," a "prominent" or "noted" educator, an "expert" on Communism; they proudly promote him as a professor (but seldom mention his poetry or English specialty). Root contributes articles to *American Opinion* (monthly voice of Robert H. W. Welch, Jr., president of the John Birch Society), *American Mercury, Human Events, Education Information, Inc.*, of California, and other ultra-conservative publications. He has spoken to enthusiastic audiences in more than a dozen states from coast to coast. His name and his writings have been cited in every major textbook battle of recent years. The Mississippi legislature hired him as an "expert" to investigate subversion in textbooks and an Illinois legislative committee called him to testify on a textbook censorship bill.

Root's role as a militant rightist contrasts sharply with his early background as a devout Quaker and pacifist. The son of a Congregational minister who at one time was head of the Massachusetts and Rhode Island Federation of

Churches, Root was twenty-two years old when the United States entered World War I in 1917. As a conscientious objector, he did not serve in the Armed Forces, a fact he recalls ruefully today: "If I had it to do over I would fight — although I still feel, politically speaking, we made a mistake getting into the war."

Brought up in the Providence, Rhode Island, area, Root graduated with an A.B. degree in 1917 from Amherst College, where he studied under Robert Frost, a poet he idolizes and mentions frequently. After a year as an English instructor at the University of Missouri he studied at Andover Theological Seminary; then, in 1920, he joined the faculty of Earlham College in Richmond, Indiana.

Throughout the twenties and most of the thirties Root considered himself a liberal, writing articles for such publications as *The World Tomorrow* and the *Christian Century*. "My education occurred," he says, "when I found in the late thirties that modern liberalism was coming to mean liberal government, not liberal man."

Root recalls that his relations with some of the other faculty members at the Quaker college began to deteriorate in the forties when the campus trend was toward liberalism and he was swinging farther to the right. But it was not until the fifties, when he made public charges of widespread Communist influence in higher education, that his colleagues began to disdain and avoid him. Root had written the charges in conservative publications and had told a Congress of Freedom rally at Omaha, Nebraska, that he believed there were about one thousand out-and-out Communists teaching in American colleges and a much larger number of dupes and fellow travelers doing the work of the Communist party in the schools.

As Root himself says, he soon found himself ostracized. He reflects on this with some self-pity now, casting himself in the role of martyrdom: "They didn't question my sincerity at Earlham; they thought I was intellectually lacking. If you're not very tough, if you can't stand being alone, don't be a conservative at a college. After a while you begin to feel something like a leper." But was Root a conservative or a reactionary?

The July 30, 1952, issue of *Human Events,* a Washington, D.C., publication, carried Root's first blast at his fellow educators. In an article titled "Darkness at Noon in American Colleges," Root wrote: "When will the American people waken to the academic status quo? Only they can change it – by refusing to send their sons and daughters to places where they will be deliberately infected with the polio of collectivism. What we need is a new revolution of 1776 – against the Tories of Collectivism, the Red Coats of Socialism. Until then American colleges will remain factories turning out robot collectivists, centers of darkness at noon."

In the same article he wrote that a majority of college professors had "allowed themselves to be captured by a ruthless, militant minority, as free Russia allowed her true revolution to be captured by a minority of red fascists, or as free Germany allowed herself to be captured by a minority of brown fascists." The nation's colleges, Root continued, "today are dominated by would-be People's Commissars for the Suppression of Wild Flowers." He described the academic climate as "aggressively collectivist."

The *Human Events* article, reprinted in the *American Legion Magazine,* stirred up the rightists and brought Root a flood of fan mail, and soon he was back in the Washington publication with this observation on the banning of a troupe of folk singers, the Weavers, from singing at a state fair: "There was the usual stupid uproar not only among 'liberals' (whose conflict with communism is always a lovers' quarrel), but even among naively ignorant conservatives."

More fan mail followed, and Root's success in recruiting followers through what he liked to do best – writing – led him to thinking in more grandiose terms, perhaps even a book on the threat of Communism in colleges. Then Root received a call he considered "providential, as if my book was fated." What happened was that Devin Garrity of Devin-Adair Company, New York, publisher of ultra-conservative books, had read "Darkness at Noon . . ." and called Root with an offer to publish a book on the subject.

Accepting with a flourish, Root told of his plans in an interview with a Dayton *Daily News* reporter, and mentioned that he had been approached by a foundation which insisted on anonymity but would underwrite his project. The article quoted Root as saying that Communism in education had an "influence more widespread than people realized" and that not only was Communistic theory being passed from teacher to pupil, but "teachers who are conservative and students who are conservative are outnumbered and often denied voice and freedom."

In a letter to the *Daily News,* Root took exception to a mention that he was "the recipient of one of the more unusual grants in this country. It is mysterious by nature, since the donor insisted on anonymity." Root wrote that because of a provision in the grant he could not name the foundation, but he said it was established by a St. Louis businessman "nobly humble and religious." His explanation did not placate his critics. Letters from other faculty members questioning the secrecy of the grant and the purpose of Root's project began appearing on the college bulletin board.

The *Daily News* took editorial note of Root's earlier charges about Communism in American colleges and questioned whether he could live up to his promise that he would investigate and "see what the truth of the matter is and then say it objectively and fairly." Had not Root already learned what he claimed to be the truth? The newspaper observed it was "a big order for a scholar who approaches his task with prejudgments as violent as those with which Prof. Root's previous writings bristle."

At the time Root himself estimated that eighty-five per cent of the country's educators were opposed to investigations such as the one he planned to undertake. But to a man like Root this apparently afforded more evidence of what he already knew anyway – that a majority of college professors followed the doctrines of collectivism – a word he sometimes equates with Communism.

Undaunted by the opposition he said he knew he faced, Root took a year's leave from Earlham College and plunged into his project. His "investigation" consisted mostly of compiling information from old newspapers and the *Congressional Record,* dragging up frayed charges of rampant Communism – charges which had been refuted or never proved. To hardly anyone's surprise, the resulting book, *Collectivism on the Campus,* published in 1954, reaffirmed Root's thesis.

The book was a slow seller and caused little excitement, but it did arouse the interest of some rightists. One was a Chicago attorney and member of the Evanston, Illinois, school board, Ira E. Westbrook. And once again, "as if by some providential act," Root was on his way to writing a book, and this one was destined to create a furor from coast to coast. Westbrook, "disturbed" by the content of high-school history textbooks in Evanston, asked Root to analyze them and see if his results would make a book.

Brainwashing in the High Schools, billed as an objective analysis of eleven American history textbooks which "parallel the Communist line," written by Root and published by Devin-Adair in 1958, quickly became the bible of ultraconservative groups which attack texts, and catapulted Root into the forefront of the assault on public education, a position he occupies with relish. (Root reported his *Collectivism on the Campus* had sold only 12,000 copies by 1962, but *Brainwashing in the High Schools* had exceeded 20,000.)

The thesis of Root's new book was that the United States was losing the Cold War and that the blame rested with history textbooks which "brainwashed" students by distorting the truth and indoctrinating them with collectivist ideas.

The book drew immediate fire from the Evanston Township High School and the Evanston American Legion post, and was challenged in many quarters, especially in the academic world. But it was ammunition for the wrath of the right and even received surprisingly good reviews from some reputable publications (for example, *Wall Street Journal,* Cincinnati *Enquirer,* Houston *Chronicle*).

Root's qualifications as an historian and dispassionate critic might be brought into sharper focus by a statement of some of his beliefs, which he expressed emphatically in an interview with an author of this book. These are his words:

JOHN F. KENNEDY—"I believe Kennedy and his administration are even softer on Communism than Eisenhower was. Kennedy is following a path of collectivism which parallels Communism and while parallel lines never meet, when they extend far enough they get into the same areas."

DWIGHT D. EISENHOWER – "He is just muddleheaded and has a lack of intelligence; he does not have the wrong will. He just doesn't know better. He was soft on Communism."

FRANKLIN D. ROOSEVELT – "He increasingly will be deflated in history; he did not have a fundamental grasp of reality, never really quite understood what it was all about."

GEORGE WASHINGTON – "The greatest President without a doubt. He was truly the father of his country."

THOMAS JEFFERSON – "He was great, too, but the liberals are trying to take him over as one of their own; if he were alive today he would not be on their side, he would be a member of the John Birch Society. He was against taxes and coercive control by the central government."

ELEANOR ROOSEVELT – "She is the typical muddleheaded liberal. She's got a soft heart, but a soft head, too."

GENERAL DOUGLAS MACARTHUR and ROBERT FROST – "They are the greatest living Americans."

SENATOR JOSEPH MCCARTHY – "He was not a genius and not a great man, but he was a great patriot and great American. He did a fine job that had to be done, and he finally worked at it so hard it killed him. The Senate censure broke his heart, but not his spirit. He was smeared and attacked in much the same manner as the John Birch Society because he was getting close to something in his investigations."

JOHN BIRCH SOCIETY – "It is one of the most consecrated and anti-Communist groups we have. It has been effective, too, and that's why it has been so viciously attacked and smeared. I'm not a member, but it's not because I don't agree with their principles. I'm just not much of a joiner. But the Birch Society is performing a great service for the country."

ROBERT WELCH – "He has great wisdom and courage. He should not have said Eisenhower was a Communist agent because that went beyond the facts, but we all make mistakes and our enemies always try to play them up instead of looking at the good we do. I was sorry to see the *National Review* and Buckley [William F. Buckley, Jr., editor] go out of their way to attack Welch and the Birch Society. Welch and his group get down to the hard, dirty in-fighting that Buckley doesn't relish."

FLUORIDATION – "I regard it as poison. It has been proved in many cases. It's a dictatorship to force people to drink fluoridated water. I won't go as far as some and say it's part of the Communist conspiracy to take over America, but it's odd and not quite a coincidence that the Communists are one hundred per cent for it. I've seen the *Daily Worker* and other Communist publications and they are one hundred per cent for it, and a pretty good working rule is that what the Communists are for is not very good for us. They uphold what weakens America."

MENTAL HEALTH – "A good psychiatrist might be all right, but mental health is something people on the other side might use to put people who disagree with them in a mental hospital. They could have banished them to a mental hospital in Alaska under one bill they had in Congress. Psychiatry is sometimes pushed to a lunatic extreme."

QUAKERS – "I still belong to the Quakers, but I'm not a pacifist any more and I don't approve of many things the Friends do – like the American Friends Service Committee.

Actually the committee's support comes ninety per cent from outside the Friends and the committee is not controlled by the Friends."

Root believes that while Communist influence has pervaded almost every walk of American life, "the inarticulate mass at the grass roots level has antipathy to Communism which has been kept silent because the liberals have usurped the megaphone. Collectivists dominate in magazines and television, intimidating right-thinking Americans. But things are slowly changing and the liberals are becoming quite frightened."

Root looks on his anti-Communist role as being fraught with physical danger and says a friend, an ex-FBI agent, warned him: "Look out for arson and mayhem; you can't tell what might happen." The professor says he is "leary of strange things and strangers" and he recalls that in 1952 a suspicious-looking fish peddler kept coming around his house, "but nothing ever came of it." Speaking quite seriously, he says: "I'm almost chagrined that I have not been attacked; maybe they think I'm not worth it."

Root's thinking may also be better understood by a brief look at some of the organizations with which he has been associated. (When one of the textbook publishers attacked in his book mentioned that Root had been connected with these groups, Root replied, "These are all patriotic groups, whose only 'guilt' is the sin of being conservative.")

Root has served as a member of the Board of Directors of the Congress of Freedom, Inc., with headquarters in Omaha, Nebraska, and was listed as a member of the Resolutions Committee when it met in convention at Biloxi, Mississippi, in April, 1957. Although he protests it is a "monstrous smear" to depict the Congress of Freedom as anti-Negro and anti-Jew, the November, 1957, issue of *Freedom Facts,* published by the organization, contained an article which listed among its "enemies" the National Association for the Advancement of Colored People, "an organization not of Negroes, but of Jews and left wingers that would drive a wedge between the Negroes and whites of the South and do untold harm to both races"; and the Anti-Defamation League of B'nai B'rith "that has builded a gestapo and engendered more hate and misunderstanding, based on falsehood, than any other organization in America." The same issue also attacked the National Council of the Churches of Christ. Root defends the Congress of Freedom as a group of "devoted and courageous American citizens who strive to preserve our Constitutional Republic."

In the fifties Root was listed on the Board of Governors of the National Council for American Education, the anti–public-education group formed by Allen A. Zoll, whose hatemongering had long been a matter of public record. Root says he resigned from the council's board "when I found out what Zoll stood for. I still believe the council was sincere in trying to promote conservative education, but it got on the sinister fringe and I don't want anything to do with anti-Semitism or racism."

Root also has been associated with the Church League of America, which has fought public education, made flagrant charges of Communism in education and distributed material attacking both the National Education Association and the National Council of Churches. Root has defended the League as "an association of laymen and ministers that stands for conservative principles." As late as 1962 the Church League, with headquarters in Wheaton, Illinois, was promoting Root's *Brainwashing in the High Schools,* and other anti-textbook material. The chairman of the League, Edgar C. Bundy, is author of *Collectivism in the Churches.*

In 1957 Root was named a member of the National Advisory Board of a coalition of rightist organizations, "We, the People!" It advertises "Booklets to Help Save America," including one on the "record of votes by our Senators and Congressmen, on socialistic issues as selected by the Americans for Democratic Action including Walter Reuther, Eleanor Roosevelt, Hubert Humphrey, Reinhold Nieber [*sic*] and other radical liberals." The group announced at its 1957 convention its purpose to tell "how difficult it is to reach and alert the brainwashed masses of America today because of the left-wing blackout covering much of the nation's press. How current programs of the federal government are propagandized and how patriotic programs to block socialism and a world police state are censored from the press, radio, TV."

In 1958 Root was listed as a member of the National Board of Fellows of the Freedom School, Colorado Springs, Colorado, whose president, Robert Le Fevre, has gone so far as to sound the alarm on *The Girl Scout Handbook,* taking exception to passages dealing with the United Nations and the League of Women Voters.

Root has been a textbook reviewer for America's Future, Inc., of New Rochelle, New York, since it established Operation Textbook in 1958. Although this group takes a more sophisticated approach than most of the others in the fight to rewrite texts, it prints and distributes propaganda attacking the Supreme Court, public education, the income tax, Social Security and organized labor. The organization is backed by business and industrial leaders, a fact that is reflected in its reviews of schoolbooks.

Root has lectured at Harding College in Searcy, Arkansas, which he terms "an excellent place doing a great job." The college was described by the New York *Times* as "perhaps the most prolific center of aggressive anti-Communist propaganda in the United States." The *Times* reported that Harding officials fear that "thousands of Communists" already have infiltrated American institutions and that the officials view the problem of combating Communism as almost entirely a matter of domestic rather than international strategy.

When Root's *Brainwashing in the High Schools* first appeared, the academic world dismissed it as a rather crude, unscholarly joke. But it was grist for the ultra-conservative propaganda mills, which cranked up for a nationwide assault that eventually forced educators to take notice. Meanwhile, Evanston, Illinois, shattered the book locally.

A scathing denunciation came from Dr. Lloyd S. Michael, Evanston High School superintendent, who released a public statement titled "False Statements about Evanston Township High School Found in *Brainwashing in the High Schools.*" The document did not deal with Root's criticism of the textbooks' contents, but it enumerated six instances in which Root was accused of committing significant errors or of distorting the facts about the school.

"We're not getting excited about the attack," Dr. Michael told newsmen. "In 1954 a special committee of our thirty-three-member lay advisory council reviewed all of the American history texts used in the school. The books have been carefully considered by the staff and the board of education, and we feel they are the best books available."

Dr. Michael noted that one of the eleven books Root cited "has never been listed for or used in United States history. It is not even an American history textbook." And he said, "As for Root's statement that another text was adopted after private individuals had exerted pressure, that is an outright lie." (Root had written in his book that one of the texts, the only one of the eleven he gave any significant favorable mention, "was added to the Evanston High School list because individuals demanded a book that did not so grossly follow the leftist line as did the others in use.")

"As for Mr. Root's book," Dr. Michael said, "we take the point of view that in this country a man is entitled to write a book on anything and if he can get it published, that's all right too. In fact, we have purchased twenty-five copies of Root's book. Our library catalogued it Monday, and copies will go to all school board members, will be placed in every American history room and in the library."

The chairman of the Evanston American Legion post's Americanism Committee finished off Root's book locally. He excoriated the professor for selecting material out of context and hurled back at him the charge of "paralleling the communist line."

Pointing out that the eleven texts were used in eight to ten thousand schools in the United States – many for as long as a quarter of a century – the Legionnaire declared: "It seems far-fetched to believe that all the publishers and their staffs, all these schools and the elected boards of citizens in charge of them, all those superintendents, and the army of teachers could be misled for all these years. . . . We tolerate in this country a rather wide divergence of views on politics and history. This is one of our freedoms. Irresponsible attacks on our own American institutions are in themselves subversive of our efforts to keep America a free country where the truth can be taught and where opinions can be freely expressed. Communism is opposed to these freedoms. To subvert the freedoms of America is to parallel the efforts of communism."

But across the country it was a different story. Root and his book got a big boost from many newspapers and ultra-conservative groups. The vigilant Daughters of the American Revolution, ever fearful of "un-American" activities, took up the cry against textbooks, and soon published its own mysteriously authored list of one hundred and seventy "objectionable" texts. Daughters and members of other groups began popping up to protest history texts at school board meetings throughout the nation.

The fact that Root was an English professor and a poet, rather than a historian and an expert on Communism, the fact that this was his first effort at historiography, and the fact that the accused authors were, as Root himself acknowledged, "reputable and famous scholars," mitigated any immediate fear that the book would have any appreciable effect. And it was perhaps because of this that educators at first were inclined to laugh off his efforts as ludicrous. But the very fact that Root was a college professor – of any kind – gave him an aura of authority to much of the public. And while ultra-conservatives often are suspicious of professors, when an educator voices views similar to their own, they tend to place implicit faith in him. Root was identified by many newspapers as a "noted" or "prominent" educator with no mention that he had taught English and not history, and some newspapers were so taken with his charges that they embellished on them, building the bugaboo of Communism to embrace school officials and teachers as well as textbooks. And so it was that Root, riding the crest of a wave of resurgent conservatism which included the rise of such organizations as the John Birch Society, became a singular figure in the war on textbooks.

Neither an historian nor a college professor was required to spot glaring distortions and meaningless methods used by Root to reach his conclusions in *Brainwashing in the High Schools.* If a text devoted more lines of copy to liberal Presidents than conservative Presidents, it was evidence of brainwashing. If it gave more pages to reporting a liberal era than a conservative era, this was further proof. As Paul Simon, an Illinois legislator and newspaper publisher, commented, "By this easy method you can measure subversion by the inch." Even Root's counting system was distorted in some instances, and Ginn and Company pointed out that his page count of thirty-nine to twenty-one in favor of the New Deal era over the Revolutionary era in Muzzey's *A History of Our Country* actually should have been forty to twenty in favor of the Revolution.

Another Root criterion was counting the page references listed in the indices. Root referred in his book to his old teacher, Robert Frost (who he now says "used to call me his best student at Amherst"), as "our one indubitably great poet," and was perturbed that the texts mentioned Carl Sandburg's works more frequently than Frost's.

Root began his book with the conclusion that history texts like those he examined were in some way responsible for the fact that many American soldiers succumbed to brainwashing in Communist prison camps. The fact is that a large percentage of the soldiers who did yield never got through high school (eighteen of the twenty-one who became "turncoats" were not graduates).

Throughout his book Root questioned the motives of the textbook authors. At one point he wrote: "These authors and these texts are not Communistic. Why then do they parallel the Communist line?" He left the question dangling and rambled on to another subject. One author was accused of "demagoguery and historical nonsense," another of falling "into Marxian terms that attack the nature of the free enterprise system," and another of slipping in "loaded questions." A broad complaint was that "many of the texts gloat over the lapses of the spirit and the evils of the flesh that have inflicted the United States. . . ."

Root complained because the texts "cited as authorities" Frederick L. Schuman, Vera Micheles Dean, Philip C. Jessup, Carey McWilliams, Matthew Josephson, Robert G. and Helen M. Lynd, Lee Huberman, Howard Fast, I. F. Stone, Max Lerner, W. E. B. Du Bois, Gunnar Myrdal and Gene Weltfish, "all of them known to sophisticated minds as collectivists."

"Leaving aside the more drastic collectivists," Root's book continued, "all the authors refer students to prevailingly 'liberal' historians." He identified them as Arthur M. Schlesinger, Jr., Henry Steele Commager, Allan Nevins, Walter Lippmann, Claude A. Bowers, Merle Curti, Herbert Croly, Stuart Chase, J. A. Magruder, John K. Fairbank, Foster Rhea Dulles, Henry Wallace, Professor Fred Rodell, of Yale, Norman Cousins, Zechariah Chafee, Jr., James A. Wechsler, Edgar Snow, O. K. Fraenkel, Vilhjalmur Stefansson, George Seldes, Herbert Agar, George S. Counts and Robert E. Sherwood.

Textbook authors and publishers denied most of Root's charges point by point, some adding scornful comments about his methods of evaluation. Here are examples from two of the publishers:

Ginn and Company on Muzzey's *A History of Our Country* –

Charge: A line count of the index shows greater space devoted to Democratic than to Republican candidates: Coolidge, 3; Hoover, 13; Wilson, 21; Franklin Roosevelt, 16; Lincoln, 12.

Reply: Lincoln, Coolidge and Hoover were single-term presidents while Wilson served two terms and Roosevelt was elected for four. Coolidge and Hoover were peacetime presidents while Wilson and Roosevelt led the nation through two world wars. Lincoln actually gets much more space in the text than Root's index count reveals. And Root errs in giving Coolidge only three index lines when the index actually shows eleven lines. An examination of the index of Mr. Root's book shows these "strange" disproportions: American way of life, one page; Communism, 18 pages; Freedom, 2 pages; Collectivism, 19 pages.

Charge: All the authors refer students to prevailing "liberal" historians, such as Arthur M. Schlesinger, Jr. (Harvard), Henry Steele Commager (Amherst-Columbia), Allan Nevins (Columbia), Merle Curti (Wisconsin), etc.

Reply: Mr. Root's list of "liberal" historians reads like a roster of the American Historical Association – of which Professor Curti is a past president and Professor Nevins [at that time] the president-designate.

Charge: Not one text mentions authorities like Freda Utley, Richard Walker, John T. Flynn, Harry Elmer

Barnes, Admiral Robert A. Theobold, William Henry Chamberlain, Max Eastman, or David Dallin.

Reply: The scholarly authors of the high school texts appear unanimous in not considering our poet's "authorities" to *be* authorities.

Houghton Mifflin Company on Canfield-Wilder's *The Making of Modern America* –

Charge: None of the eleven textbooks in American history makes it clear that the government of the United States is a republic, not a democracy; none of the texts lists the word "republic" in its index.

Reply: Strangely enough the word "republic" does not appear in the Constitution either. Section 4 of Article IV does state that "the United States shall guarantee to every State in the Union a republican form of government. . . ." Canfield and Wilder do refer to the government founded under the Constitution as a republic on page 138, page 160, and twice on page 203. An index is a convenient and time-saving tool, but it is hardly an infallible basis for leveling grave charges against a book of over seven hundred pages.

Root branded the publishers' replies "utter nonsense," but he was offended by one which charged that he had used writing tactics usually associated with making a "fast buck." "That was a rather awful thing for them to say," says Root. "I write these things because I believe in them, not to make money. I have made a respectable sum, but I'm not getting rich. Conservatives don't make money writing; you have to be a liberal. The publishers' answers didn't make much sense – they just said the authors were fine scholars and I was an ignoramus and a rascal."

In a New York *Times* review, William H. Cornog, superintendent of New Trier Township High School, Winnetka, Illinois, criticized the book and Root's methods of evaluation. And a review in *Social Education* by Erling M. Hunt, professor of history at Columbia University Teachers College, began: "This book is a phony. Ostensibly concerned because schools don't teach the author's kind of patriotism, it is actually a diatribe against government regulation of business, the welfare state, foreign aid, and any interference with what Root calls the free enterprise system." "His methods and his findings," wrote Hunt, "mark him, rather than his intended victims, as truly subversive of American scholarship and patriotism."

Edwin C. Rozwenc, professor of American History at Amherst, Root's alma mater, declared in the *Amherst Alumni News* that Root showed a "wonderful array of private prejudices" and that his "anxieties over the left-wing character of American history textbooks reduce him to counting the number of lines in the indices. . . . He is outraged to discover that Jefferson gets more lines than Washington, and seems to think there is something sinister in the fact that Calvin Coolidge receives only thirty-five lines compared to Franklin Roosevelt's one hundred and fifty-one."

Why, after such ridicule from publications of the stature of the New York *Times, Social Education* and the *Amherst Alumni News,* would anyone be beguiled by Root's book? The fact is that in many cases the book got favorable mention. To thousands of persons the book came as an ominous alarm, especially when accompanied by such dire warnings as those of the New York *Daily News.* With one of its subheadlines reading "Poison in Textbooks," the *News* printed in a lengthy lead editorial a list of the books Root examined, then apologized: "Sorry to take up so much space with that list, but it's an important one. These books are widely used in American schools." The tabloid pointed out that the New York City Board of Education sends a list of a "large number" of history textbooks to each high school principal and lets him choose which of these are to be studied in his school. "Obviously," cried the *Daily News,* "if a principal happens to be a Communist, Fascist, Socialist or America-is-no-gooder, he can force textbooks that peddle his particular ideology on his defenseless pupils, and rule out books which truly and patriotically tell the great American story. There are many of the former and few of the latter."

In Texas, where some of the bitterest textbook battles have been fought, the Houston *Chronicle* was just as worried as the *Daily News* about "brainwashing" material Root had detected. It carried a review headlined "Distortions in Textbooks Feed Treason to Pupils," which concluded that Root had provided "sufficient answer" to the question of why so many Americans in Korea succumbed to brainwashing. A column by Harold G. Pyle in the same edition, headlined "How History Textbooks Are Brainwashing American Youth," exclaimed: "No wonder our youth is filled with false ideas and no solid grounding in Americanism."

The Pawtucket, Rhode Island, *Times* was a little more cautious, but nonetheless worried: "If our children's knowledge of history is poisoned at the source, as the Evanston survey suggests, a textbook housecleaning in our American schools would not be amiss."

And so it went across the country. Some newspapers apparently reviewed Root's book and accepted his charges without question, without checking the texts of which he wrote. At his critics the professor hurled the fact of favorable reviews: "Three-fourths of all reviews (including the Wall Street Journal, The Tablet of Brooklyn, the Cincinnati Enquirer, the Indianapolis Star, etc., etc., and critics like Forest Davis and Holmes Alexander) have been favorable."

Root was on his way now, and, as a National Education Association memorandum noted, his book had "stimulated other groups and persons to call for censorship action in all branches of school work. Proposals cover fields from American history to zoology and suggest action from book-burning to labeling of 'dangerous' books."

In the wake of Root's book, the Daughters of the American Revolution issued its incredible report condemning one hundred and seventy books, and America's Future, Inc., launched its textbook reviewing service with Root as one of the reviewers. These three elements – Root and his book, the DAR and America's Future – quickly became the dominant forces in the fight to censor school books.

Textbook controversies erupted in New York, California, Texas, Oklahoma, Georgia, Alabama, Arkansas, Ohio, Illinois, Michigan, Mississippi, Virginia and other states.

Copies of Root's book were mailed to Illinois legislators prior to the opening of their 1959 session and Root appeared before the state Senate Education Committee to argue for a textbook censorship bill. The measure provided for a system of evaluating school textbooks on the basis of whether they were "antagonistic to or incompatible with the ideals and principles of the American constitutional form of government."

Root suffered a crushing defeat here as he had in Evanston. Senator Bernard S. Neistein, Chicago Democrat, called the move "trying to fight communism with fascism." Senator Marshall Korshak, another Chicago Democrat, said, "the evaluating committee would usurp the powers of the local school board" and "it would create psychological warfare. . . . We are becoming more like the Russians when we engage in this type of legislation." And a Republican from Evanston, Senator W. Russell Arrington, said he personally knew two of the textbook authors Root criticized and "they're one hundred per cent Americans."

But the most devastating attack on Root's book came from Ray Allen Billington, professor of American history at Northwestern University. Billington studied all eleven textbooks and Root's book, then appeared before the Senate Education Committee and submitted a lengthy written report which, the Chicago *Sun-Times* said, "effectively refuted" Root. Billington said that by using Root's techniques of quoting out of context he could go through the same texts and draw opposite conclusions, showing that "their authors distort history to uphold the glories of conservatism, the virtues of the Republican Party, the evils of the New Deal, and terrors of communism." He rebuked Root for insinuating that the textbook authors "have connived together or are under the direction of some Moscow-inspired force bent on undermining popular faith in the nation."

Billington's blistering report did not spare the textbook publishers either. He wrote: "Nearly all of these texts are conservatively oriented in that they are less expressive of a particular viewpoint – either liberal or conservative – than most college texts. This is because all attempt to hew close to the factual line with little interpretation or expression of value judgments. As a result I found most of them dull.

Many, in addition, are poorly organized, and a surprisingly large number are unaware of some of the latest trends in historical research. Deficient as they may be in scholarship or sparkling prose, however, they are meticulous in their efforts to present the past fairly and without prejudice."

While the Illinois legislature rejected the bill, Root proved more successful in Mississippi, where the legislature hired him as "an expert in the field of public school textbooks and subversive writings." The DAR started the textbook circus in Mississippi, and soon got help from the American Legion and the White Citizens Council. But Professor Root was to be the main attraction. It was in Mississippi that Root introduced the term "patriotic hate" and tiptoed around the race issue.

5

The Daughters See Red

IT WAS MARCH 7, 1962. Mrs. Wilson K. Barnes, a stout, elderly woman wearing dark glasses, bustled into the National Defense Committee in the DAR headquarters building in Washington.

Three other ladies working in the main office looked up from their desks and smiled as their leader hurried by, heading for her own private office. They were paid staff members, but she was a volunteer worker, devoting her time and enthusiasm to a cause she believed would help save the country from Communism.

Mrs. Barnes was "terribly busy," she explained to an author of this book, and really had no time to talk to anyone about the mysteriously authored *Textbook Study*. She was quick to point out that she became chairman of the National Defense Committee *after* the committee had completed the study in 1959.

The textbook report was a shotgun blast at "subversion," peppering many of America's leading historians, textbook authors and publishers. The Daughters had solemnly warned that "some central source within the educational apparatus" dictated the content of most American textbooks—and they cited one hundred and seventy "subversive" volumes.

For three years now throughout the country the Daughters had been using the report to sow seeds of suspicion about textbooks. Not that this was the first time they had attempted such censorship; but never before had they issued and given such widespread and sustained distribution to accusations against so many people.

If there were a substantial degree of truth to the charges, the nation's students had indeed been inculcated with un-American ideas. In fact, if the Daughters were right, they had been subverted for twenty-five years or more, since many of the books dated back that far.

Who had leveled these charges? What were their qualifications? Were they educators? Were they "experts" on Communism? What criteria were used in evaluating the books? The National Defense Committee began distribution of the report in 1959 and the National Society, Daughters of the American Revolution, at its 1960 convention, praised the "valuable" study, but who – specifically – were the reviewers?

Mrs. Barnes reluctantly agreed to consider a few questions. "I haven't worked much on textbooks," she said. "I just haven't had time, you know, we've got so many defense projects. But it's a fine thing to do, to look into subversion in the books, and I wish I had more time to do it. But you know the administration changes every three years and every chairman has her own hobbies and everything like that."

Yes, the National Defense Committee was still mailing out copies of the three-year-old document "almost every day." No, the different organizations which had requested copies of the report would not be identified and the number of copies distributed would not be revealed. "We just don't keep those kind of records, you know," Mrs. Barnes said, "and besides our files are not open to the public or the newspapers."

No, the committee would not reveal the names of the authors of the *Textbook Study,* or even their qualifications. "The committee that made the study disbanded after the report was filed and that's all I can tell you."

Although Mrs. Barnes was not chairman of the committee which made the study, it was under her administration, which ended in April, 1962, that the report got such wide distribution. But she refused to talk about it. She did say that she "told those men in Meriden the DAR appreciated what they were doing, taking the time to look into subversion in textbooks and all that. I told them I was very happy about it and I thought they had made a very intelligent approach to the problem." And she suggested, "You go talk to America's Future in New Rochelle. They're going at the textbooks tooth and toenail and doing a mighty fine job."

Mrs. Ray L. Erb, who was chairman of the National Defense Committee when the study was made, also has refused to identify the authors of the report. After her term of office as chairman of the committee expired, Mrs. Erb began writing *Report to the Nation,* a publication of the American Coalition of Patriotic Societies. The coalition, with headquarters in Washington, is comprised of some one hundred twenty-five conservative groups claiming a total membership of around four million. It also distributes material charging subversion in texts.

That the patriotically indignant Daughters see Red in so many areas of American life is a fact to be weighed in evaluating their attacks on school books. They worry about Communist infiltration in religion, mental health programs, public schools and colleges, the Federal Government, metropolitan government, urban renewal, Christmas cards, and all international activities, including cultural interchange.

Mrs. Jacqueline Kennedy focused front-page attention on the DAR in 1961 when she publicly announced that she was buying UNICEF (United Nations Children's Fund) Christmas cards despite a DAR cry that the cards were entwined in the menacing web of the Communist conspiracy. The National Defense Committee had claimed the cards were "part of a broader communist plan to destroy religious beliefs and customs and to transfer Christianity in a 'One World Peace Festival.' " Nor was this the first time the Daughters had sounded the alarm on them. In the *DAR Magazine* in November, 1957, Mrs. Henry Deland Strack of New Jersey wrote: "That UNICEF promoted Christianity not at all, but served Moslem and Buddhist with equal blandness, is well known. Pakistan children playing, as depicted on one of these cards, had no connection whatever with Christmas." Mrs. Strack warned: "When you choose your Christmas cards, be alert to any outright or concealed technique indulged in to convey a clandestine Marxist message."

While the announcement by the nation's First Lady spotlighted the DAR's concern over Communism in Christmas cards, the Daughters' activities usually get little play in the nation's press. It is not, however, because the DAR, with its 180,000 members in more than 2800 chapters, has rested in assaying the menace of subversion. The Red threat obviously is a constant thorn in the side of the Daughters and they are forever writing and talking about it. When they are not writing and speaking about it themselves, they are distributing the writings and utterances of others who share the same fears.

In April, 1959, about the time the Daughters began distributing *Textbook Study* (except to news media), the DAR, at its annual convention, adopted a resolution opposing metropolitan area government as "a long-range, well-designated plan looking toward the ultimate establishment of a totalitarian world government." The Daughters also opposed cultural interchange with the Soviet Union and other Iron Curtain countries, and lambasted the UN Children's Fund as an attempt to "promote the world welfare state."

The DAR several times has urged the United States to withdraw from the United Nations. In 1960, the Daughters came out in favor of an Air Force manual which was withdrawn after the National Council of the Churches of Christ held it unfairly charged Communist infiltration of the Protestant clergy.

The DAR circulates a long list of literature from the John Birch Society and other ultra-conservative groups attacking mental health programs, fluoridation, the U. S. Supreme Court, President Kennedy's Peace Corps, immigration, the UN, the National Council of Churches, public education, the National Education Association, and other aspects of American life. Titles of some of the books and pamphlets the DAR distributes include: *Collectivism in the Churches* . . . *Has the Methodist Church Gone Mad?* . . . *Marxism in Christmas Cards* . . . *Metro Monster* . . . *Operation Peace Corps — "A Pig in a Poke"* . . . *Nine Men Against America* (about the Supreme Court) . . . *Cultural Exchange — Conduit for Communism* . . . *What's Happened to Our Schools?* The 1962 list of literature being distributed by the National Defense Committee included one hundred and thirty-five books and pamphlets. Thirty-nine dealt with the United Nations, fifteen with education, nine with mental health, nine with religion, five with fluoridation and four with immigration. The remainder were lumped into categories designated Constitution and Constitutional Rights, nine; Communism and Socialism, eleven; World Government, six; and miscellaneous, twenty-eight. Practically every piece evidences the Daughters' fears of Communist subversion.

In November, 1958, shortly after E. Merrill Root's *Brainwashing in the High Schools* was published, the DAR began quietly compiling a list of textbooks used in state primary and secondary schools throughout the nation. When newsmen in Connecticut learned that Miss Barbara F. Allen of Norwich, the state's National Defense chairman, had requested a list of texts from the school superintendent, they asked her for comment. "I can't tell you the reason for it," she said, "except that I am carrying out instructions of our national headquarters in Washington." The brief notice of Miss Allen's request apparently was the only public mention of the DAR's work until after copies of *Textbook Study* had been distributed from coast to coast in early 1959—and even then the publicity was sporadic, originating in scattered localities as DAR chapters began protesting the use of "unsatisfactory" texts.

The Daughters had not released information on the document from their national headquarters in Washington, and thereby had escaped the attention of the nation's press and other news media. In fact, the *Textbook Study* itself, although of unquestionable public interest, has never been reported in detail for a national audience. There have been no definitive articles on it in any of the magazines of general circulation or on any of the wire services. As a consequence, when a DAR chapter drags out the old report for a censorship fling, the local community usually is hearing the charges of rampant subversion for the first time. It is not aware of the DAR's secretive handling of the project, it does not see the full findings, and it usually does not know of the Daughters' tendency to see Communism in almost every area of American life.

To show the scope of their inquiry, the Daughters declared in *Textbook Study* that lists of texts used in states from coast to coast "were carefully studied and a sampling selected. Every well-known textbook publisher was represented; many of the books were on numerous recommended state lists."

Of two hundred and fourteen volumes examined, only fifty met "minimum DAR standards" and some of these were criticized. Five of the books listed in *Brainwashing in the High Schools* made the DAR "unsatisfactory" category. The Daughters' document, which promoted the sale of Root's book, also listed the other six texts to which he had objected.

The DAR reported, "The general design and purpose of every textbook were weighed in the light of the excellent prior study made by the Sons of the American Revolution in 1949 entitled 'A Bill of Grievances,' to determine if our young students are emphatically taught love of God and Country or are being corrupted to accept socialism and materialism."

While Root had stuck to textbooks in history, the Daughters branched out, unearthing what they considered subversion even in books on music, geography, arithmetic, biology and literature. "In music," according to the DAR report, "too many 'work tunes' and 'folk songs' (as distinguished from native and national airs) were found. One of the tools promoting the 'class struggle' is the emphasis upon songs of the 'burden bearer,' 'the tenant,' the 'downtrodden' (always ignoring the heavy responsibilities of the managerial and professional classes, of course). Communist and union songbooks feature many such whining tunes."

For each of the fifty volumes found "satisfactory," the Daughters listed brief specific "reasons." A civics book was praised for "special mention of the nobility of Washington's character." DAR accolades were also won by a geography text for having "no left-of-center propaganda"; by a world literature anthology for being " 'international' only in the sense that it represents a sampling of world literature"; and by a music book for the "absence of agitational songs." Some of the volumes got only conditional approval. One was marked satisfactory except for "several propagandists in the bibliography" and another was found to be of "excellent quality" but "reviewer assumes from generally sound treatment that authors included through ignorance several left-of-center writers."

"Since the number of books that proved unsatisfactory is much greater and the reasons would make too lengthy a report," the *Textbook Study* explained, "they are listed only by title, author and publisher." Thus, one hundred and seventy texts were lumped together with "an analysis of general reasons for rejection," all being identified and branded un-American by the DAR.

"General reasons" for rejection by the Daughters included that the books: (1) treat "our Christian heritage warily" and are "guardedly patriotic"; (2) show a "perceivable pattern of 'economic determinism' "; (3) leave the impression with the reviewer "that some central source within the educational apparatus directs and dictates what textbooks must emphasize"; (4) describe the United States as a democracy rather than a republic; (5) "emphasize the Bill of Rights rather than the original instrument, the Constitution"; (6) fail to warn students that "the government does not 'provide' anything except what it dispenses from the taxpayer's pocket"; and (7) include too much "realistic literature."

The books also were accused of "playing up to the vanity and discontent natural to the young . . . an accepted technique of the radical left." The Daughters discerned a danger of subversion in lowering the age for voting rights to eighteen, something the state of Georgia did almost twenty years ago. "In the 1940s," the Daughters warned, "the Communist-dominated National Citizens Political Action Committee and later the Progressive Citizens of America advocated voting privileges for those eighteen years of age. Later, Americans for Democratic Action took up the refrain. In his October 4, 1958, column, Louis Budenz exposed the detailed plan recommended in the Communist monthly, *Political Affairs,* for renewed Marxist activities in youth organizations, *advancing the Communist line as non-Communist proposals* to affect the youth of our land."

The Daughters found that in the texts "fear and compromise are developed by the inclusion of numerous pacifist writers, by the featuring of photographs of mushrooming nuclear bombs, by recommending such books as John Hersey's *Hiroshima.* This negative approach can only result in paralysis of the will through fear which is known in psychological warfare as Soviet Principle Ten. Mao Tse-tung calls it 'psychological disintegration.' The only solution, according to this type of 'fear' text, to the problem of atomic warfare is the surrendering of our national sovereignty to a world government. In fact, many writers for the United World Federalists are suggested in reading list after reading list: Carlos Romulo, Dorothy Canfield Fisher, Brock Chisholm, Carl Van Doren, Russell Crouse, Norman Cousins, Cass Canfield, Edgar Ansel Mowrer, Oscar Hammerstein II, James P. Warburg and even foreign-born propagandist, 'Emery Reeves' (Emery Reves). Thus, the One Worlders are placed in a strategic position to 'engineer consent' by influencing the minds of our future voters."

Perhaps the most important discovery, according to the *Textbook Study,* was that "while the Rugg and Muzzey books have faded into the background (after long-time opposition by patriotic and veterans' groups), the viewpoint represented by the Frontier Thinkers and by the progressive educationists is now promoted by dozens of their disciples under the slogan 'THE FUSED DISCIPLINES.' By this dazzling flight into semantics, the propagandists in our educational system have coined a meaningless term designed to obscure. Basically, a discipline exists as an organic whole. To 'fuse' it is to blur it making the subject less clear. In the fused disciplines, therefore, we come upon a mixture of history, geography, civics and personal guidance that prevents the students from acquiring a clear concept of national boundaries, or of the great and cumulative differences of one civilization over another—for example, the difference between the achievements of the Igorots and of the Greeks."

The books are "guilty of special pleading from the liberals and internationalists," according to the DAR report, because writings by the following persons were listed for supplementary study: "Ruth Benedict, Gene Weltfish, Carey McWilliams, Shirley Graham, and her husband, W. E. B. Du Bois, Theodore H. White, Alan Lomax, B. A. Botkin, Osmund Fraenkel, Matthew Josephson, Joseph Gaer, Louis Dolivet, Henrietta Buckmaster, Langston Hughes, Otto Klineberg, Emil Lengyel, Maxwell S. Stewart, William Gropper, Louis Adamic, Margaret Mead, Gordon Allport, Henry P. Fairchild, Corliss Lamont, Nathaniel Peffer, John K. Fairbank, Clyde R. Miller, T. A. Brisson (T. A. Bisson), Bernard J. Stern, John A. Kingsbury, Margaret Halsey, Frederick L. Schuman, Harry W. Laidler, Lynd Ward, Burl Ives, Albert L. Guerrard [*sic*], Lincoln Steffens, Louis Untermeyer, Millicent Selsam, Alexander B. Novikoff, Lawrence Rossinger, Howart Fast, Richard Wright, Vilhjalmur Stefansson, Bill Mauldin, Sidonie Gruenberg, Wm. C. Menninger, Albert Deutsch. The records of these persons are available from the House Committee on Un-American Activities upon the request of your Congressmen."

The Daughters lumped the following sources, all listed in the books covered in the *Textbook Study,* in a category labeled "Liberal, racial, socialist or labor agitators": "Harold Laski, Morris Ernst, Herbert Agar, Henry Steele Commager, Allan Nevins, Carl Carmer, Mark Starr, Vera M. Dean, George S. Counts, Harold Lasswell, Willard Goslin, Frank Magruder, Zechariah Chaffee; such publications as those of the Public Affairs Committee, the 20th Century Fund, Foreign Policy Association, Fund for the Republic, Freedom Agenda (distributed by the League of Women Voters); and such other sources as the National Lawyers Guild, Council Against Intolerance, Bureau for International Education, National Labor Service, Brandon Films and Teaching Film Custodians."

The *Textbook Study* concluded with a plea that all DAR chapters use it to fight the textbook battle, to see that "unsatisfactory" volumes were replaced with ones that met with the DAR's approval.

Thousands of copies of the report were distributed throughout the United States to DAR chapters and other ultra-conservative organizations and individuals. While the National Defense Committee would not reveal how many had been circulated, the committee reported in 1961 a mailing list of 6923 names, including "many nonmembers interested in our resolutions and documented reports."

The American Library Committee, in its December, 1959, *Newsletter on Intellectual Freedom,* taking note of the rash of textbook battles, warned of the strong trend of censorship and declared: "Of all the programs by organized groups, the DAR textbook investigation, at both national and state level, was the most specific and . . . the most threatening."

In North Carolina the state medical society and the American Legion reacted swiftly to endorse the Daughters' report. The society also overwhelmingly approved a committee report that branded some textbooks as "radical and objectionable," and accused the National Education Association of having "a virtual monopoly over courses of study and educational programs in the public schools." The physicians voted to bring pressure both locally and at the state level.

And in the North Carolina legislature, Representative Rachel Davis, a physician, introduced a bill to put eight laymen on the state commission that approves textbooks. A committee killed the bill after educators testified against it. One school superintendent told the lawmakers that educators were greatly concerned over the increasing attacks on public education. "God knows," he said, "it's hard enough now to get young people interested in the school business. School people are not going to let socialism and Communism creep into our schools." Another superintendent said the list of authors condemned by the DAR "reads like a *Who's Who* of American Literature." The Raleigh *News and Observer* commented: "The worst charge aimed at the State Textbook Commissioner during a public hearing yesterday was that school children aren't getting the 'beautiful poetry' that some parents so well remember."

The DAR scored its most significant successes in Mississippi and Texas, where the Daughters gained the support of other ultra-conservative organizations and of sympathetic legislators. In these, as in some other Southern states, segregationists jumped at the chance to tie the race issue to a hunt for Reds.

With the aid of the American Legion, the White Citizens Council, and the Farm Bureau in Mississippi, the DAR, waving a list of forty-four "unsatisfactory" volumes used in the state's schools, brought about a legislative investigation in 1959. The Daughters demanded that watchdog laymen be put on the teacher committees which were commissioned by the State Textbook Purchasing Board to screen books.

In the audience to assist the General Legislative Investigating Committee when it met at Jackson to look into "subversive" textbooks was a group of DAR ladies led by Mrs. Harry Artz Alexander of Grenada, the spirited chairman of Mississippi's Defense Committee, who later spoke in Texas to promote censorship efforts in that state. Also backing up the legislative committee were two White Citizens Council officials and Myers E. Lowman, of Cincinnati, Ohio, executive director of the Circuit Riders, an organization founded by a group of Methodist laymen to fight subversion.

Jay Milner, a newspaperman formerly of Greenville, Mississippi, writing in the New York *Herald Tribune,* took note of the Citizens Council efforts to censor textbooks: "While the more overt aspects of white Mississippi's campaign to maintain segregation are hitting the headlines a more sinister manifestation of the struggle is growing quietly in the heat of that state's emotional involvement. White Citizens Council leaders have often expressed the realization that, as one put it, 'the weakest link in our solid front of resistance is our youth. They are so impressionable.' Apparently with this in mind some Mississippians have set out to purge all levels of education in the state of influences that might tilt the status quo."

The Mississippi legislators failed to detect as much subversion as the Daughters had reported. They trimmed the DAR's list to twenty-seven books, then decided they did "not feel qualified to make the necessary study and analyzation [*sic*] of these texts and, therefore, sought the advice . . . of a person qualified to perform these services." The committee reported it was "fortunate in securing the services of Mr. E. Merrill Root . . . who was confidentially recommended to your committee by an unimpeachable source as an expert in the field of public school textbooks and subversive writings."

Root, who received a four-hundred-dollar fee from the state of Mississippi for his two weeks' work, labeled twelve of the books satisfactory, twelve unsatisfactory and three mediocre. The Root findings became the committee report with the added recommendation that, "unless there be reasons to the contrary," all texts marked unsatisfactory and mediocre "should be eliminated from further use in the public schools in Mississippi."

Root, obviously pleased to have his doctrines embodied in an official state document, added to his usual charges a spark of rhetoric: "In understanding the dangerous influence of superficial textbooks, we must first realize that our danger as a nation today lies not primarily in outward military attack but in inward subversion of our values. . . . Thus our real battle is not so much of bullets as of brains – not of missiles but of minds – not of weapons but of wills – not of space but of spirit. Whatever weakens our wills and confuses our minds will overthrow us more surely than do the tanks that roll or the bombs that fall."

Then he got to the heart of the matter: There is "too much" of Lincoln Steffens, Arthur Miller, Archibald MacLeish, Carl Sandburg, Arthur M. Schlesinger; tendency to interpret the American Revolution in terms of a class war; authors praise government aid and control; authors accept the income tax with acclaim; exaggerates American extremes of wealth and poverty; will leave students in a pink political fog; authors are too glib and naïve; the Nazis are blackened, the Communists faintly whitewashed; "reform" is overemphasized.

The English professor criticized the authors of one history text for writing that the Rumanians had a "grudge against the Russians." Root thought the term should have been "patriotic hate."

And Mississippi offered the chance to expand on his preference for his old teacher, Robert Frost, and his disdain for Carl Sandburg. Of the latter, he wrote: "too loosely and sentimentally liberal and a much over-rated poet . . . artistically slipshod . . . such minor writers as Sandburg,

Steinbeck and Dorothy Parker." While approving one history book, Root warned that its "weakness" was that "the introduction is written by the democratically sentimental Carl Sandburg." At one point Root did concede that Sandburg himself was not "subversive" and that a poem of his included in one of the books was "quite harmless."

Root reiterated objections to writers he named in *Brainwashing in the High Schools* and added these to his list: Hodding Carter, Eleanor Roosevelt, James B. Conant, Karl Shapiro, William O. Douglas, Malcolm Cowley, Oscar Hammerstein II, Walter Lippmann, Jacob K. Javits, H. Hubert Wilson, Sidney Hook, Robert M. MacIver, Joseph S. Clark, Leland Stowe and Reinhold Niebuhr.

The usually vitriolic Root treated the race issue rather lightly and ambiguously, apparently hoping to assuage the segregationists of Mississippi while not appearing an ally. Here is what he said of one book: "The authors believe that schools, to promote the democratic spirit, should be a 'melting Pot,' 'modifying many of the differences in children of varying cultural, racial and economic backgrounds.' But schools inevitably will do that; and, if they do it in wise ways AND WITHOUT FORCED INTEGRATION, it will be good. Certainly it is not subversive to suggest this. We may differ – I do NOT differ personally – on this matter; but it is not subversive or destructive for these authors to state their own humane and democratic views." Root wrote that "the book does not anywhere . . . uphold racial intermarriage or 'complete integration' by force."

Following its committee's report, the 1960 Mississippi legislature took up a DAR-backed bill to eliminate "subversive material" from texts by taking control of the textbook selection committees from the superintendent of education and giving it to the governor. The measure touched off a bitter fight with Governor Ross Barnett pushing for enactment and former Governor J. P. Coleman, a member of the House of Representatives at that time, spearheading the opposition. "You can find things in the Bible you don't like but there has been no bill introduced to ban the Bible," Coleman declared. But the chairman of the House Education Committee argued: "There are too many outside influences coming into our state." He suggested Mississippi might do better by establishing its own printing press for textbooks. Another legislator said Mississippi would have escaped the controversy if it had heeded the late Governor Theodore Bilbo's recommendation in 1928 and established a state printing press to keep "foreign ideologies" out of school children's minds.

The Mississippi Education Association adopted a resolution opposing "investigations of our textbooks made by irresponsible parties. We do not believe that one authority living in another state should judge the fitness of textbooks selected by well-qualified and intelligent teachers of our state. Our association condemns such book purgings which are, in effect, expressions of a lack of confidence in the integrity, loyalty and good judgment of the teachers of Mississippi." The Mississippi School Administrators Association labeled those attacking the books as "witch-hunters."

Although badly outnumbered, the professional educators' champions in the legislature were outspoken. One saw the bill as a "direct slap" at the teaching profession and added: "I voted to starve them [on a pay-raise bill] but I'll not come down here and insult them." He said, "I had rather trust them than some of the people I have seen hanging around the governor's office looking for jobs." And another warned his colleagues: "You are setting into motion the greatest juggernaut of thought control that has ever been devised by man." Representative Coleman said, "Teachers were everybody's darlings during the political campaigns last summer. But now they are being accused of everything from incompetence to ratifying subversive textbooks."

But the powerful influence of Governor Barnett proved too great to match. Barnett made a special overture to the legislature: "Failure of the House to act favorably upon this bill will, I very much fear, hamper our efforts to clean up our public school textbooks and give our children the instruction material they must have if they are to be properly informed of the Southern and true American way of life." Barnett said he had "a lot of confidence" in the DAR, the American Legion and other organizations fighting for the bill and added, "they believe there is a lot of subversion in these textbooks that should come out."

The new law empowered the governor to make appointments to the state's eight textbook screening committees. He now appoints four members to each of the seven-member bodies and the school superintendent appoints three. The superintendent previously appointed all seven and all appointments went to teachers.

While Governor Barnett's first appointments went mostly to teachers or other persons connected with education, some also went to leaders of censorship groups. His new appointees included a long-time DAR leader and the president of the Mississippi Farm Bureau Federation. One of the teachers he appointed was a Mississippi College political science professor who had spoken frequently at White Citizens Council meetings.

Mrs. Alexander, the state DAR chief of textbook censorship, told a reporter that several of Governor Barnett's appointees were Daughters and that the screening committees had frequently called on the DAR for advice on textbook evaluation.

The fifteen books condemned by the legislature – those branded "unsatisfactory" and "mediocre" by Root – were still being used in Mississippi schools in 1962. But the battle was far from over. The censorship groups returned to the attack with support of a book-burning bill that included those fifteen and twenty others. While the bill failed in committee, there was a movement to organize support for a similar measure in 1963. And in the same year the state was scheduled for a new round of high-school textbook selections – the first since Governor Barnett gained control of the screening committees.

The DAR's current censorship efforts in Texas began in 1960 and by 1962 a sweeping legislative inquiry was under way with a committee report due to be presented to the 1963 Texas General Assembly. Mrs. A. A. Forrester of Texarkana, leading the DAR charge, sounded the familiar refrain on "subversion" and in 1962 called for an investigation of all texts adopted by the Texas Education Agency.

The Amarillo Conservative Club, impressed by Mrs. Alexander's success in Mississippi, brought her to Amarillo for a speech promoted as a "help" for the Texas investigation. The club credited Mrs. Alexander and the DAR with getting beneficent legislation enacted in Mississippi. She responded by reeling off numerous charges of subversion, bearing down on textbook treatment of the United Nations which she called a "giant octopus . . . robbing the nation of its sovereignty and prestige." The audience of three hundred interrupted her eight times with enthusiastic applause.

When the Texas Daughters and John Birch Society members objected to the use of Albert Einstein's name in books, a representative for the Macmillan Company replied, "We can't change history." But in Texas the pressure groups *were* able to change some of the history books.

6

America's Future

SINCE THE FALL of 1958 the most prolific nationwide propaganda barrage against textbooks has emanated from the second floor of a small building in New Rochelle, New York. It is the headquarters of America's Future, Inc., which claims to be a nonpartisan, nonprofit educational organization, a status which exempts it from the income tax it abhors.

Most residents of New Rochelle are not even aware that America's Future has its offices in the heart of the city's business district. "You just don't hear much about America's Future locally," says Elmer H. Miller, editor of the New Rochelle *Standard-Star*. "Neither the organization nor its staff members participate in community affairs." But America's Future is known to a vast radio audience across the country; for years it has publicized its political and economic philosophy over a paid fifteen-minute program, "Behind the Headlines," broadcast every Sunday night over the Mutual Broadcasting System.

America's Future operates on an annual budget it reports to be in excess of a quarter of a million dollars. It is controlled by a group of business and industrial executives, including a member of the Council of the John Birch Society.

Three of the reviewers of textbooks for America's Future are editors of *American Opinion,* the monthly publication of Robert Welch, president of the John Birch Society. Two other reviewers have written articles for the Welch periodical, which is published in the John Birch Society headquarters in Belmont, Massachusetts. Each issue of the magazine includes this notice: "We use almost no articles except those written to order to fit our specific needs. . . ."

From the time of its establishment in 1946, America's Future has been one of the country's most vociferous agents of ultra-conservatism. But its activities against "subversion" in textbooks were sporadic until 1958 when it launched a sustained program, "Operation Textbook." Publication of Root's *Brainwashing in the High Schools* and Rosalie Gordon's *What's Happened to Our Schools?,* both distributed by America's Future, resulted in a flood of requests for textbook evaluations that could be answered, according to Rudolf K. Scott, president of the organization, only by initiating a book review service.

Scott, suave, distinguished looking, a middle-aged man with wavy gray hair, talks freely of his organization's attempts to influence the contents of textbooks. In an interview with one of the authors of this book, he pondered the phobia of Communism which usually pervades attacks on texts and, speaking slowly and intently, measuring his words precisely, said:

"No American textbook publishers have stooped to subversion. There is no evidence of that and I don't like extremism. The whole thing of liberalism in the textbooks has been an evolution, taking place over the past decade or two. But we are going to change that. We have already had some influence and we ultimately will exercise a very considerable force in textbook publishing. Publishers have had a free hand too long. There were no qualified persons criticizing them. Now we are hitting the publisher where it hurts – in his pocketbook."

Scott made the comment in an interview in March, 1962, in his office in New Rochelle, where he heads a staff of sixteen. He talked of the success of America's Future in the textbook field and of grandiose plans to expand its services to college textbooks in 1963. And the more he talked the more he tried to leave an impression that the role of America's Future was one of moderation, of education. His group eschewed extremism, he said, and really sought only to uphold its "principles of free competitive enterprise and constitutional government."

"I disapprove of scare tactics," said Scott. "This is a grave mistake that many organizations and individuals have made. You read about fluoridation being a part of the Communist conspiracy!" He hesitated a moment and chuckled for effect, then continued: "These people see bogeymen behind every closet door. Sometimes I don't know whether they are attempting to be dramatic or are sincere."

Scott said, "When we don't like something in a book, we try to tell why we think so – and we document chapter and verse. This is one area where the DAR and some others have fallen into a serious trap – I don't think that is the way to handle a subject as serious as this one. We are not trying to destroy books; we are trying to promote balanced books we think are good instruments for learning."

Scott had gone all the way now in his denunciation of

extremism and Red-scare strategy. He had ridiculed the anti-fluoridationists and he had even taken a dig at the DAR by name. But on the question of the Red bugaboo, America's Future itself has a long record to which it was still adding in 1962.

During the 1950s a onetime New Deal liberal, John T. Flynn, was its chief spokesman. Warning of socialism and the threat of Communism in the churches, in the schools, in the government and in other areas of American life, Flynn wrote numerous pamphlets for America's Future and spoke weekly on its nationwide radio program, "Behind the Headlines."

As a staff member of the liberal *New Republic* during the thirties, Flynn wrote articles highly critical of big business. In one on September 9, 1936, "The Booing Brokers of the Stock Exchange," Flynn labeled brokers of Wall Street "booing boobs." Under the title, "To Get Rich—Scare the Rich," Flynn wrote that the rich were ripe for plucking and offered this tongue-in-cheek advice to the "acquisitive writer":

"The Red Menace sparkles on every side. Raids upon his money bags are a threat on every quarter. This is a natural atmosphere for the rich man's terrors. Scare him some more. Then invent some racket for protecting him from these perils. One good field—which is the occasion of this outburst to the acquisitive writer—is the schools. There the Bolsheviki are ceaseless. They are stealing the souls of our children, poisoning the minds of our teachers. They are being taught the wickedness of wealth and undermining its constitutional props. Therefore, what better racket than to save the schools from this monster? Therefore, organize an agency like, for instance, the National Republican Lettergram Service of Washington, D.C. Send out letters, bulletins, circulars and pamphlets keeping the loyal teachers advised of the march of the Reds upon the schools. Then you can call on patriotic rich men to subscribe $100, $150, or maybe $1000 to carry on the great work. I don't know how the National Republican Lettergram Services are doing. But this is a rich territory."

Fifteen years later Flynn had lassoed a lucrative position with America's Future and was as busy trying to save the country from the march of the Red Menace as he had been ridiculing "booing brokers" and "acquisitive writers."

Although an ardent New Dealer during President Franklin D. Roosevelt's first term, Flynn, by the 1940s, had become a caustic critic of Roosevelt and had begun applying the label "social planners" to leaders of the Administration and of the Democratic Party, to leaders in labor circles, to the Federal Council of Churches (later renamed National Council), to college professors and other groups. In a book published in 1940, *Country Squire in the White House,* Flynn wrote: "The simple truth is – though Americans have not realized it – that we have a militarist in the White House who would if he dared propose it, establish an army with peacetime conscription, on the European model. . . . He is now the recognized leader of the war party."

The same year President Roosevelt excoriated Flynn in a letter to the editor of the *Yale Review*. Protesting an attack by Flynn in the *Review,* Roosevelt wrote: "I have watched John T. Flynn these many years and the net answer in my mind is that he has always, with practically no exception, been a destructive rather than a constructive force."

The cleavage between Flynn and the *New Republic,* widened by his growing isolationist stand, had become intolerable about this time and he left the magazine. In an editorial, the *New Republic* explained the breakup: "The collapse of France and the danger of possible British defeat suddenly brought home to all sensible Americans the fact that the peril was much greater and more imminent than we had previously believed it to be. We do not see how anyone . . . can dispute the fact that Hitler is a menace to this country, and to this extent, England's battle is our own. He [Flynn] is willing to take a chance that this country can exist safe and secure in a world the rest of which is dominated by Hitler and his friends. He thinks military attack is unlikely, and has such confidence in his own opinion that he is willing to run the risk that if he is wrong, this nation will be destroyed. . . . The editors of the *New Republic* do not believe in their own infallibility. . . . They are ready to admit they may be wrong: but when the existence of the country is at stake it is better to be sure than sorry."

In the forties Flynn wrote articles for Merwin K. Hart's National Economic Council and several books including one, *As We Go Marching,* which charged that Roosevelt was leading the country toward totalitarianism. He also wrote pieces for the Hearst press and together they kept up a constant clamor about communism in America.

Karl Schriftgiesser, in *The Lobbyist: The Art and Business of Influencing Lawmakers,* published in 1951, called Flynn a "renegade New Dealer, former America Firster, and articulate Roosevelt hater, whose violent diatribes, *Country Squire in the White House* and *The Roosevelt Myth,* stand out as two of the great biographical and historical distortions of our times." Schriftgiesser wrote that Flynn's associates "have collected and spent thousands of dollars to spread his doctrines through the country with the help of some of the most dangerous pressure groups of our time."

In *The Road Ahead: America's Creeping Revolution,* published in 1949 by Devin-Adair and circulated by America's Future, Flynn warned of socialist professors promoting "revolutionary objectives" in American colleges instead of sticking to teaching. And he flailed out at publishers, too: "What is true of the faculties is also true of the publishing world which supplies textbooks and college literature. A favorite roosting place for these revolutionary gentlemen is in the editorial sanctums of the textbook publishing houses."

Flynn has been a chronic worrier about betrayal of the country by Americans. Titles of some of the pamphlets and talks he has made reflect his fears: *Why Korea? Story of Blackest Intrigue and Betrayal in America's History; Trapped in Asia; Secret Espionage Cells in Washington; Hidden Documents; A Deal Cooked Up Between Acheson and Britain; Glorifying the Soviet; Betrayal at Yalta; Indoctrination on the Sly; Textbooks Are Perverted; How Can We Save Our Schools?*

From 1951 until 1959, when the radio program was taken over by Rudolf K. Scott, Flynn broadcast his weekly worries about the American Red Menace over the fifteen-minute program sponsored by America's Future. On the program he quoted such sources as Robert Welch's *American Opinion.* His fears, which he shared with a radio audience of millions, included this one: ". . . that a group of teachers – very important in the teaching profession – many of them high up in the councils of the national teacher organizations – have been carrying on a conspiracy for a number of years to use our public schools for the purpose of indoctrinating the students in the principles of socialism."

America's Future, which in 1962 was still distributing copies of many of Flynn's books, broadcasts and pamphlets, brought in a long-time paid textbook critic, the irrepressible Lucille Cardin Crain, of the now-defunct *Educational Reviewer,* to be executive secretary of "Operation Textbook."

After pledging to enter the field of evaluating schoolbooks with an open mind and provide "Authoritative, objective reviews," America's Future announced "Operation Textbook" would show that ". . . through the textbooks used in the schools, particularly in the field of the so-called 'social sciences,' the progressive revolutionaries have done their most damaging work in the past quarter of a century. But so slyly and slickly has the collectivist-internationalist philosophy been inserted . . . that it is difficult, if not impossible, for the average parent or school board member any longer to tell what is a good textbook and what is not."

So this organization of business and industrial leaders, with its long record of fierce isolationism and ultra-conservatism, was prepared to tell parents and school board members what was and what was not a good book. To do the telling it engaged the services of Mrs. Crain, two of her colleagues from the *Educational Reviewer,* and ten others, including E. Merrill Root; Neil Carothers, dean emeritus of College of Business Administration, Lehigh University, Bethlehem, Pennsylvania; Medford Evans, chairman, Department of Political Science, Kenyon College, Gambier, Ohio; Russell Kirk, research professor of political science, C. W. Post College, Long Island University; J. B. Matthews, author and lecturer and former staff member of Senator

McCarthy's subcommittee of the Senate Internal Security Committee; and Charles Callan Tansill, former professor of American History, Georgetown University, Washington, D.C. Later, six reviewers were added to the list. They included Anthony T. Bouscaren, associate professor of political science, Le Moyne College, Syracuse, New York, and Hans F. Sennholz, chairman, Department of Economics, Grove City College, Grove City, Pennsylvania.

Since publication of the first issue of Robert Welch's *American Opinion* in February, 1958, J. B. Matthews and Hans Sennholz have been associate editors with Medford Evans a contributing editor. E. Merrill Root and Russell Kirk also have written articles for the magazine.

Like John T. Flynn, J. B. Matthews is a former liberal who turned to ultra-conservative writing and lecturing as a profession. And like Flynn, he was connected with the Hearst newspapers during the forties. He was a staff investigator for the Dies House Un-American Activities Committee and later served on the staff of McCarthy's subcommittee. Matthews once collaborated with Allen A. Zoll on a booklet, *How Red Is the National Council of Churches?* They concluded it was quite Red.

In the July, 1953, *American Mercury,* Matthews wrote an article which began, "The largest single group supporting the Communist apparatus in the United States today is composed of clergymen." He charged that "some seven thousand American Protestant clergymen" had been lured into "the network of the Kremlin's conspiracy." The ministerial storm this kicked up blew Matthews right off the McCarthy subcommittee, with the Wisconsin senator "very reluctantly" accepting his resignation.

Medford Evans, who the *National Review* reported was

"a victim of conformist pressures at Northwestern College in Louisiana" when he left the college faculty as social science professor in 1960, was back in the news in 1962 as a "consultant" to the controversial Edwin A. Walker, who resigned his commission as an Army major general after being reprimanded for extreme right-wing activities. When Walker appeared before the Senate committee looking into alleged "muzzling" of the military, Evans was at his side scribbling notes to guide him. In his rambling testimony, Walker claimed he was a "scapegoat" of an unwritten American policy of "collaboration and collusion with the international Communist conspiracy."

Most of the educators reviewing textbooks for America's Future have long records as ultra-conservative leaders. All but two – Root and Matthews – are Ph.D.'s. At forty-five, Sennholz was the youngest of the sixteen reviewers in 1962. Eight had reached or passed "retirement age," sixty-five.

By late 1962 America's Future had mailed out thousands of copies of reviews of more than two hundred high-school texts. The reviews went to educators, school board members, and numerous organizations dedicated to censoring "subversion" from texts. In its pamphlets America's Future stresses that its evaluations are available free of charge.

While they unquestionably are more scholarly and more specific in their criticism than the textbook evaluations of the DAR and other rightist groups, through them runs a similar theme protesting material on the income tax, Social Security, TVA, liberal authors, labor unions, the United Nations, Democratic Presidents, and so forth.

And this "educational project," which according to America's Future provides "authoritative, objective reviews," is not above sending out a review of a book written by one of its own staff.

Two of the busiest reviewers, Medford Evans and Russell Kirk, who have had articles in the same issue of *American Opinion,* also wound up together in an America's Future review. This was Evans's evaluation of Kirk's *The American Cause,* published by Henry Regnery Company, Chicago, in 1957, one of the sweetest reviews ever to flow from the New Rochelle office: "This book is one in a million, and one that a million have wanted. It ought to be a textbook in every high school in the country." Evans went on at length in the same vein and admitted the purpose of his review "unabashedly is to get Kirk's book adopted as a text in as many American schools as possible." Evans wrote that the book explains "eloquently, but more important, simply and clearly – the principles our country stands for, and on."

Of most textbooks, of course, America's Future is hypercritical, and the reviews sometimes include pleas that the readers use as textbook material some of the ultra-conservative material it distributes from New Rochelle.

Bouscaren found fault with one volume because the bibliography on Russia and eastern Europe cited John Gunther and Eleanor Roosevelt and did not "counterbalance" them with William H. Chamberlain and David Dallin. In another review, he wrote: "Elmer Davis, Edward R. Murrow, Howard K. Smith and Eric Sevareid are described as 'well-informed and politically literate commentators.' Further, the authors might have included in their description of those named 'liberal' and 'left-wing.' All have tended to be 'understanding' of the USSR, and have favored labor over business. All have been critical of Congressional investigations into Communist activity." Bouscaren also objected because students were referred to *Reader's Guide* for sources, thereby being deprived "of much anti-communist and pro-government information such as is found in *New Leader* and *Human Events* for these publications are not indexed in the *Guide*."

Sennholz, reviewing an economics book, *American Capitalism,* objected because "the radical government intervention bordering on socialism is not even mentioned. No mention is made of the numerous schemes of re-distribution of wealth and income, the confiscatory taxation of large fortunes and incomes." In the same review, Sennholz complained: "No mention is made of the minimum wage legislation that keeps millions of Americans unemployed, or the ever rising unemployment compensation that destroys the incentive to work. The booklet fails to mention the feverish sequence of economic booms and recessions, accompanied by a feverish legislative activity that is breeding radical interventionism and socialism." In another review, Sennholz wrote: "The United Nations must fail, like the League of Nations has failed, because it lacks the spirit of genuine capitalism." He recommended to readers of the review Orval Watts's *The United Nations: Planned Tyranny,* published by Devin-Adair in 1955.

Kirk objected to a book's frequent favorable mentions of what he called the "god-term 'democracy.'" He wrote that a "besetting vice of democracies is their tendency to submerge the individual in the mass; aristocratic republics are far more concerned for individuals." Kirk complained that the work had "small space for heroes, or for high deeds" but "a great deal of space for discussion of the rise and importance of state schools. Education is a god-term, like

'Democracy,' so that there are twenty-nine references to 'Education' in the index – some of these extending to several pages in the text."

Of another volume, Kirk wrote that it contained a "confused and sentimental notion of democracy," but added it did make an "attempt at representing the less fuzzy views of popular government; short selections, for instance, from George Washington, Jefferson, Webster, Lincoln, Charles Evans Hughes, and Winston Churchill. (But none from John Adams, John Quincy Adams, John Randolph, John C. Calhoun or Theodore Roosevelt – though Langston Hughes, Franklin Roosevelt, Frank Murphy, David E. Lilienthal, Archibald MacLeish, Arthur M. Schlesinger, Jr., and Charles Bowles are given their say.)"

In one review, Carothers made an all-embracing charge against textbooks for their material on labor unions: "This milk-and-water treatment of the grave problem of union power is inevitable. No book which deals frankly with unions can hope for adoption in any public school. This book goes about as far as it can go. This reviewer knows no college economics text which tells the truth about unions. For that matter, it may be said that the solution of the union problem does not lie in textbooks."

Tansill criticized a text for not indicating the "many failures" of the United Nations. His review concluded with a sentence which implied he expected some compliance from the publisher: "There are serious errors of omission which mar the later chapters of this textbook, but these can probably be rectified in a later edition."

The secretary of America's Future is Rosalie M. Gordon, who served for more than twenty-five years as research associate for John T. Flynn and whose writings bear this out. In *Nine Men Against America,* she recommended that all decisions of the Supreme Court from 1937 to the present "should be declared to have no force and effect as precedents in judicial or other proceedings in determining the meaning of the words, sections and provisions of the Constitution."

In *What's Happened to Our Schools?,* Miss Gordon wrote: *"No one who has watched closely what has been going on in our public school system in America these past two decades can escape the feeling that something drastic — and rather terrible — has happened to it. What is more, it is difficult to believe that it has happened by accident, that there has not been a planned, slyly executed and almost successful attempt to deliberately under-educate our children in order to make them into an unquestioning mass who would follow meekly those who wish to turn the American Republic into a socialistic society."* (The italics are Miss Gordon's.)

Who foots the bill for the propaganda mill at New Rochelle? Rudolf K. Scott, the former North Carolina radio station executive who became president of America's Future in 1957, claims that "primarily our funds come from Mr. Average Citizen. Contributions are small for the most part, $15 to $20 each. Ninety-five per cent of the funds are personally solicited through the mail."

A look at the names of the trustees of America's Future would indicate, however, that considerable financial support is available from that source. All are executives of big firms. Scott refused to reveal the source of all funds and he said he could not permit the authors of this book to examine the minutes of the organization's trustee meetings. America's Future advertises that contributions to it are deductible from income tax in accordance with a Treasury Department ruling.

A former trustee is General Robert E. Wood, the onetime Board Chairman of Sears, Roebuck and Company. He was an early organizer of the pre–World War II isolationist movement known as the "America First Committee." After the war he was publicly identified with organizations hostile to the United Nations. Robert L. Lund, of St. Louis, Missouri, a former president of the National Association of Manufacturers, was president of America's Future at the time of his death in 1957.

America's Future had expenses reaching $265,599 during 1961, according to a report by Robert F. Montgomery, Certified Public Accountant. The report showed the organization's income totaled $251,927, which included $177,645 in contributions; $16,603 in the sale of books; $30,292 in sale of "special pamphlets"; $18,978 in subscriptions to the newsletter, and $4429 for mailing list rental.

The budget for "Operation Textbook" in the fall of 1960 designated $22,138 for "an introductory mailing to a list of 218,000 social science teachers, school board members, PTA officers, high school principals and school superintendents. Each mailing to consist of covering letter, check list of books evaluated, reply envelope. Cost of lists, enclosures, postage, etc." The budget earmarked $10,000 for "handling and mailing of requested evaluations, including postage, envelopes, clerical work, etc."

America's Future formerly was located in New York City, where, according to Rudolf Scott, it "shared some equipment" with the Committee for Constitutional Government. But Scott contends this is the only connection his group has ever had with the Committee, an arch-conservative lobbying group. America's Future is extremely sensitive on this point because on its claim of being a nonpartisan, nonprofit educational organization rests its tax-exempt status.

Literature from America's Future has turned up on textbook battlegrounds throughout the country. While the organization itself does not send representatives to school board meetings or other sessions where textbook adoptions are discussed, its publications are used by the John Birch Society, the DAR, some local American Legion posts, and other groups which fight the war at the local level.

With America's Future planning to accelerate its textbook campaign and enter the college field in 1963, and with other ultra-conservative organizations stepping up their assaults on textbooks in the sixties, where does this leave the liberals?

"At this point the liberals don't need to review books," says America's Future president, Rudolf Scott. "They are well represented in the books. But there's no question but that there eventually will be a liberal organization doing it."

Meanwhile, fed by such propagandists as America's Future, textbook critics have been busy across the country, and nowhere have they enjoyed it so much and tasted so much success as in Texas. There material from America's Future, the DAR and other national organizations has been used to prevent adoption of texts, and to rewrite some textbook passages and expunge others.

7

Hell of a Fellow

EXCEPT FOR HIS EDUCATION and elocution, J. Evetts Haley could have stepped from the pages of W. J. Cash's classic study, *The Mind of the South*. He fits almost to a fault that rugged frontiersman Cash so appropriately described as a "Hell of a fellow." He is daring, dogmatic, damning, and a stringent segregationist. He talks tough. He once wrote that he was "born to battle."

Because of his fondness for patriotic symbols, it is a pity his birth did not come a day earlier. Born in Belton, Texas, July 5, 1901, James Evetts Haley claims two Confederate veterans as grandfathers – a Mississippi planter on the paternal side, a Texas "trail driver" on the maternal side. When he ran for Governor of Texas in 1956 he also included on his campaign literature: "great-grandson of James Evetts, veteran of the Battle of San Jacinto; raised at Midland, Texas, in the Methodist Episcopal Church, South!"

Haley rode the range as a boy, punching cows in the Pecos Valley around Midland in West Texas. Later he went to West Texas State College and the University of Texas for his B.A. and M.A. degrees, and began research for his first book, *The XIT Ranch.* The volume, the first of ten he was to write on cowboys and ranch life in the next quarter of a century, appeared in 1929. The same year he accepted a research post in the university's history department. He remained for seven years, becoming so bitter with the New Deal during that time that he finally asked for a leave of absence "to fight the Roosevelt regime." When the request was rejected, he accused the university of "firing me by inaction."

In 1936, the year he left the university, his biography of a cowboy, *Charles Goodnight, Cowman and Plainsman,* was published by Houghton Mifflin Company of Boston. His long-time friend, J. Frank Dobie of Austin, a well-known historian, called it "one of the finest books on a cowboy ever written."

Haley began ranching now near Canyon, Texas, and letters he wrote to Dobie reflected his bitterness with the university, which he never forgave, and his acidic antipathy to the New Deal, which he still loathes. They also showed his warm friendship with Dobie and his chagrin that other colleagues had deserted him.

He wrote of having spoken his mind "upon our plethora of demagogues" and of having been "quite unhappy to see friends whom I had cherished for years, and for whom I have sweat and hoped, dropping by the trail because they lacked the character to belly up to the lick log. Well, I fought the battle of my convictions, and for what I know is right, and I hope that I fought it like a real Texan. . . ."

Dobie, meanwhile, had been trying to secure another college position for his friend, but Haley, denouncing "intellectual bastards," wondered whether he could ever again adjust to academic life. His feelings were so strong, he wrote, that he might be driven to "do violence to somebody if he has enough manhood to resent an insult."

Haley's letter cited his own "violent views on individualism" and asserted that the "only place" for him at that time was the country. His impression was that "if the present tide of mass emotionalism keeps running, outright revolution is not far away." And he felt that in this event, he would be "among the first to be liquidated, for I do not intend to compromise the love of freedom for any political son of a bitch."

Haley thrived on the rugged ranch life and six months later wrote Dobie of accepting a job to "straighten out the outfit" working a vast ranch in Arizona. He found the place "one hell of a mess" with a hundred head of cattle in the corrals and no feed on hand, the boss "talking big and practicing with his six-shooter when not running into town and back, and irresponsibility generally branded over the whole outfit." With great relish, he wrote how he himself pitched in and washed pots and pans and did other menial chores while, at the same time, he took inventory and "stocked the place with Texas cowpunchers, bought some more horses, weaned the last year's calves, read the riot act on occasion, and made a night drive from the ranch into Phoenix to catch the man who had been handling the place and put him on the spot, which I did."

The ranch was "underdeveloped" and the "sewerage arrangements would make Mrs. Roosevelt start another rural rehabilitation project." But Haley and his men were "telling the federal boys to go to hell with their range programs, and as for plumbing, we are using the same that cowboys have flourished on since the beginning of the cow country."

Haley soon became general manager of more than 300,000 acres of range operations in Arizona, New Mexico and Texas. In Gallup, New Mexico, his habit of working alongside the cowhands almost cost him his life when he was severely trampled in a stampede. But he was soon back in the saddle and operating his own outfits on the Pecos, Canadian and Arkansas River ranges.

Meanwhile, he continued his running diatribe on the Roosevelt administration and found time for writing several articles and books on cowboys and ranch life. He was well known in Texas now as a historian of the ranch and in 1950 was elected president of the Panhandle-Plains Museum at Canyon, and later was named a trustee of the National Cowboy Hall of Fame. He also had made a name for himself among cowboys for his fearless bronco-busting. In 1951, Dobie received a letter from a friend saying he had read Dobie's article on mustang taming and just wanted to say he had seen Haley "tame an outlaw that had defied breaking for four years—had thrown every rider who attempted to ride him and was vicious besides. Haley did this in three hours. . . ."

Although long active in politics, Haley did not seek public office until 1956 when he announced for governor. He obviously knew his chances of victory were nil, but the candidacy gave him a forum to vent on the electorate his anger at the Supreme Court's 1954 decision outlawing segregation in public schools.

Haley ran a blunt-spoken campaign on a strong states' rights platform, the major plank being a proposal to interpose Texas sovereignty as a means of defying the decision. "I'm for its use to stop this mixing of white and Negro children in public schools with its consequent destruction of our race and our way of life," he declared at a rally. He said if he were governor and a U. S. Marshal tried to enforce integration orders, he would "send a Texas Ranger to meet that marshal and arrest him and throw him in the hoosegow. That, my friends, is interposition. I expect to interpose."

When a CIO representative asked him his attitude toward labor, he retorted: "I believe that you have the same right to organize that anybody else has, big business or little. I believe you have a right to quit work whenever you want to. But if after you do quit you think you have the right to keep somebody else off the job, let me tell you this: If on my ranch a bunch of hands quit and you fellows come up there trying to interfere with the people I then hire to flank a bunch of yearlings on my land, I'll meet you at the fence with a .32 and, if necessary, I'll draw a bead on you and rim a shell and leave you lying on the fence line. If that isn't plain enough, I'll make it plainer."

Haley's plain talk got him a surprising number of votes, 88,772, but he finished a distant third in a field of three, with Prince Daniel winning with 628,941 votes.

In 1959 Haley was back in the headlines hurling epithets at the Supreme Court on a more personal matter. His son, James Evetts, Jr., also a rancher, had been penalized $506 for growing forty-three acres of wheat without an allotment from the U. S. Agriculture Department. Young Haley had won the suit in federal district court, but the government appealed to the Supreme Court where he was ordered to pay. This proved too much for the senior Haley, who called the federal farm program "legalized, collective theft," and told newsmen: "Apparently nobody can get consideration of his constitutional rights in this country from the present Supreme Court unless he is a Communist, a Negro or a foreigner." He referred to "predatory government" and said his son faced a "tragic dilemma — to stay in this country and change his profession, or submit to this damned tyranny."

Haley, still calling himself a cowhand while operating his own 11,000-acre ranch near Canyon, now concentrated his wrath on a field he had forsaken — education. Wearing tailored rodeo suits and cowboy boots, he showed up at State Textbook Committee hearings as president of a newly organized right-wing group, Texans for America. He also unleashed an attack against Southern Methodist University, but found more opposition there than he was to encounter in his textbook forays.

In January, 1960, Haley boasted that Texans for America had distributed to alumni and students' parents more than eight thousand copies of an *American Mercury* article claiming that SMU was tainted with left-wingers. The article charged that "leftism's most familiar masquerade is internationalism" and that "its principal base of operations in Dallas is the Southern Methodist University." University officials charged the magazine and Haley with perpetrating a malicious smear. Dr. Willis Tate, the president, said, "We have never attempted to dignify this article by comment because it is filled with obvious untruths and malicious deceit."

The student newspaper, the *SMU Campus,* lashing back at Haley, questioned the "credibility" of the witnesses. It reported the *Mercury,* which has been one of the ultraconservatives' favorite outlets for attacks on books, was owned by Russell Maguire, a rich manufacturer, who was found by the Securities and Exchange Commission to have willfully violated the Securities Act.

Haley also made headlines at another college by punching a professor. A history instructor, John W. Cooke, attacked the credibility of the movie, "Operation Abolition," after it was shown at West Texas State College at Canyon. An argument ensued when Cooke claimed the film implied that anyone who disagreed with the House Un-American Activities Committee was a Communist sympathizer. Despite his age, then sixty-one, the lean, leathery Haley lit into the thirty-six-year-old Cooke, and newspapers reported that J. Evetts, Jr., also entered the fray. The next day Haley, Sr., told newsmen that Cooke had called him a liar and "I might be quoted as confirming the fight."

The counterattack by SMU had snuffed out the furor there, and the Texans for America now trained all their guns on one of the biggest textbook markets in the world. Texas schools purchase from six million to ten million dollars' worth of texts a year. The state Textbook Committee approves five books in each course, leaving the local boards to choose any one. The approved list for each course remains in effect for six to nine years.

Haley, a spellbinder whose flowing rhetoric and histrionics smack of the old-time revivalists, was just the cataclysmic force for which the DAR, certain American Legion posts and other rightist groups had longed in their efforts to incorporate their own brand of patriotism into the school books. And the Texans for America drew heavily on the DAR, the Legion and the John Birch Society for members. Among them were Medford Evans, reviewer for America's Future and organizer for the Birch Society in Louisiana and

Texas, and Mrs. A. A. Forester, chairman of the DAR National Defense Committee in Texas.

Haley made clear part of his criteria for evaluating the volumes: "The stressing of both sides of a controversy only confuses the young and encourages them to make snap judgments based on insufficient evidence. Until they are old enough to understand both sides of a question, they should be taught only the American side. . . ."

And he frequently combined his attacks on school books with bitter tirades on the Supreme Court. Some two thousand rightists cheered lustily at the National Indignation Convention in Houston in 1962 when he tore into textbooks and Chief Justice Earl Warren. Introduced as a "great patriot" by Tom Anderson of Nashville, Tennessee, a member of the National Council of the John Birch Society, Haley declared: "I'm a newcomer to the ranks of the book burners. I'm called a witch hunter. Well, I'm not so worried 'bout witches, but I sure am worried about some of these sons of witches. . . ." The crowd roared in laughter. "Tom Anderson here has turned moderate," Haley continued. "All he wants to do is impeach Warren – I'm for hanging him."

In one of his newsletters, Haley expressed yet another fear, that the public-school guidance and counseling program "threatens to become a gigantic mental health program for the suppression of the individuality of every child to make him a cog in a socialistic society. . . . It is for the indoctrination of your child, into a groove selected for him in advance by hand-picked servants of the Super State."

Haleyites criticizing history books bitterly opposed favorable mention of the income tax, federal subsidies to farms and schools, the TVA, Social Security, unemployment compensation, labor unions, the United Nations, the League of Nations, racial integration, General George Marshall, the Supreme Court, and on and on – practically the same list used by other ultra-conservative censorship groups. At the same time they demanded more favorable treatment for Herbert Hoover, the "traditional" presentation of Christianity, the "traditional" stories of national heroes, Senator Joseph McCarthy, Chiang Kai-shek, General Douglas MacArthur, and the rest.

With the help of propaganda from the DAR, the Sons of the American Revolution, America's Future, the American Legion, the Church League of America of Wheaton, Illinois, the National Anti-Communist League of San Gabriel, California, and the Parents for Better Education of California, the Texans for America served notice on the state Textbook Committee that they would have to be reckoned with before any books could be adopted. Haley said some two hundred Texans were working on the matter.

At one committee hearing Haley tore into a volume for listing Ralph Bunche as a "distinguished statesman" and neglecting "to say he is reported to have 12 Communist front citations and many other things." He called Bunche, the United States Undersecretary for Special Political Affairs, a "willing tool of this international conspiracy to destroy us."

When he made a similar attack on Langston Hughes, the publisher replied, "Langston Hughes is an internationally known Negro poet whose accomplishments in the field of letters have been recognized by such awards as the Harmon gold medal for literature, a Guggenheim Fellowship for creative writing, a Rosenwald fellowship. . . ."

Haley said this only proved "the degenerate nature of the people who decide these awards." The committee later bowed to Haley, ruling that Hughes's name and works would have to be deleted from books bought for Texas schools.

Although Texans for America has among its members a sprinkling of attorneys, former teachers and others who, like Haley, are college graduates, it registers some of the most fantastic complaints ever lodged against texts. Some of the Texans themselves have worried lest they appear to be crackpots. One of them, R. A. Kilpatrick of Cleburne, who described himself as a "country lawyer," told the committee:

"Now I know some of you think that we are just a bunch of crackpot radicals that don't know what we're talking about, and that we are scared, which we are. But I think it is wise to gamble. I always as a lawyer try to warn my clients of any approaching danger. Then if it doesn't happen, my judgment is just bad, and they just think I am a nutty lawyer; but if I happen to be right, why, then they have a different attitude. So we are scared. I am. If it turns out – and I'm not scared of Russia, I am scared of America – if it turns out I am wrong, it is just another crackpot lawyer; but if it turns out I am right, then think of the eventuality. What if we are right?"

Kilpatrick went on to object that Upton Sinclair, Jack London, Ida Tarbell and Lincoln Steffens "are listed in the book as 'young novelists who wrote powerful stories about the evils around them' – then it gives the title of each book or books and tells what it is written about. I call it promoting the writings of known subversive writers. Not only that, the publisher and author of the textbook put pictures of both London and Steffens in this book. . . ." He also protested that there was only one mention of Will Rogers and said, "It is interesting to note that at the end of the chapter, the student is not asked to gather additional material on Will Rogers. Guess he was *too American* for the author of this textbook!"

A Corsicana woman invoked the name of "the noted Professor E. Merrill Root" and went on to castigate a history book for eliciting "the students' acceptance of socialistic and world-involvement trends."

And Dr. Don I. Riddle, a veterinarian appointed by Haley to head the Texans' textbook committee, deplored the "trend . . . of pointing out all of the faults and the human frailties of our founding fathers and men who were instrumental in forming this country." He said he was not denying the facts, but questioned whether the facts should be reported. He also objected "unequivocally" to a passage which said that because the Ku Klux Klan was American-bred, it, more than Communism, was an "enduring blot" on the United States.

Dr. Riddle accused the book of "approaches of character assassination" of Senator McCarthy and protested this passage: "The fear of Communist infiltration and espionage had foundation, but reckless Red-hunters, led by Senator Joseph R. McCarthy of Wisconsin, exaggerated the number and influence of the Communists in Washington and threw the nation into angry confusion."

One of the most apprehensive witnesses was Mrs. Joe A. Slade of Fort Worth, who detected a loophole in the Texas law requiring textbook publishers and authors to sign a non-Communist oath. "I might remind you," she solemnly warned the committee, "that an oath as we know it is sworn under God, and atheist factions would not be bound by an oath." Her fears included: "Now the Communists are using words to defeat us. We are being influenced daily, moment by moment. Now Americans would not choose Communism, if we had a choice we would not choose Communism, but we are being influenced, and our children can be molded to fit into the mold of Karl Marx and we will not realize what has happened."

Haleyites also complained that a history text contained four pictures of George Washington which "lacked his familiar features of kindness and dignity." They charged that one, though done by a contemporary of Washington, "looks as if George Gobel posed for the painting." Another charge, made with grim determination, was that the song "He's Got the Whole World in His Hands" smacked of one-worldism.

The DAR, led by Mrs. Forrester, was forced into a supporting role by the drive and enthusiasm of Haley and his Texans. The former schoolteacher assured herself of some of the censorship glory by joining the Texans and declaring she stood solidly behind Haley.

Altogether, the Texans objected to fifty of the books up for adoption in 1961. The Daughters criticized four of these as well as another text.

Occasional errors of fact were detected in some of the volumes, but the minute constructive corrections were submerged in a torrent of accusations and cries for censorship of sentiments obnoxious to the complainers.

The Texans and the Daughters, fortified with propaganda from numerous national organizations and supported locally by the John Birch Society, some American Legion posts, and the Sons of the American Revolution, operated with little opposition. The publishers did little more than to file written answers to the charges, refuting most of them by showing that the words in question had been quoted out of context or otherwise misrepresented. Since the few reporters at the committee hearings were not furnished with copies, the public remained no wiser.

Only one publisher fought back face to face. The Webster Publishing Company was stung into action when Haley not only attacked one of its authors, Dr. Paul F. Boller, Jr., history professor at SMU, but attacked the publisher as well. Haley accused Boller of being "soft on Communism or short on logic and learning, or perhaps both" because the teacher had publicly stated that the Communist party is "practically defunct in this country and is an irrelevant reference of importance." He charged that Webster had collaborated in publishing Communist propaganda because early in World War II, under a contract with the Federal Government, the firm had published a pamphlet about Russia which was circulated among the Armed Forces. A representative of the Webster Company accused Haley in return of resorting to "mendacity, thought-control and character-assassination." (Despite the Texans' objections, Boller's book was one of five adopted by the State Textbook Committee for a history course. However, Boller later contended that the attacks, which continued at the local level, seriously curtailed sales. School boards which might have preferred his book selected one of the others to avoid further controversy.)

Another publisher was so overwhelmed that his texts had escaped condemnation at a committee hearing that he could only express gratification at the proceedings. "I was very pleased to note our books were not criticized at all in today's meeting," said Kendrick Noble, of Noble and Noble, Publishers, Inc. "I think this is one of the most wonderful meetings I have ever attended. Democracy in action, and I think so many of these men and women came so far to get better books in schools."

For the most part Texas newspapers did very little comprehensive reporting of the censorship efforts, just as later they did practically nothing to report the success of the censors. The only thorough coverage and strong editorial denunciation came from the scrappy *Texas Observer,* a weekly published in Austin. The *Observer,* which enjoys a select circulation among politicians and educators, including many out of the state, reported the hearings in detail and lampooned the censorship groups.

In the words of *Publishers' Weekly,* the book industry journal, "Newspapers paid but scant attention to the textbook hearing – only two Texas dailies and one weekly sent reporters – and not even the book publishers seemed to be especially concerned, for relatively few defense witnesses spoke – so few that Reporter Bob Sherrill of the liberal *Texas Observer* . . . remarked, 'It was about as poor a job of public relations as I've ever seen. The press heard the fanatics' full voice, but heard hardly a chirp from the publishers.' " Sherrill also commented that the publishers were operating in an "atmosphere of frantic commercialism" and that they showed "an eagerness to sail with the wind of strongest opinion."

When the State Textbook Committee, on October 5, 1961, approved fifty books for adoption, including twenty-seven the Texans had opposed, some newspapers pointed to this as a defeat for Haley. But the *Observer* pointed out that records in the Texas Education Agency would show otherwise. In the first place, the committee had rejected a dozen books the Texans had opposed, and it had turned down four of the five books condemned by both the Texans and the DAR. Furthermore, the committee had bowed to the critics to some degree on all books that were approved, and had ordered substantial changes in specific ones. Except for the *Texas Observer,* the press did little to report these facts.

One member of the State Textbook Committee believed "we held our own" with the censorship groups. J. B. Golden, director of the Textbook Division of the Texas Education Agency, was quoted by the *Observer* as saying: "By golly, they [the Texans for America] had some basis for their criticism. Some of the things they pointed out as needing changed had already been caught by the members of the State Textbook Committee, but some other things they caught on their own, and the committee felt they made good sense."

The files of the Education Agency reflect only some of the alterations. Some were agreed on orally in closed-door discussions between the committee and the publishers, and there is no public record of these. The committee does not actually "order" modifications; it recommends; but the publisher must comply to make the adoption list. When a reporter was checking the TEA files, a secretary in the Commissioner of Education's office told him, "The competition is so fierce, you know, that the textbook publishers are anxious to make any changes the committee recommends."

The committee itself questioned the motives of one publisher, Lyons and Carnahan, whose eagerness to please the critics was all too obvious. In its report on the firm's book *Freedom's Frontier,* the committee noted that the only objection had been to "its reference to seven persons whose loyalty had been questioned." The report continued, "In their reply the publishers say, 'Assuming that the committee is right in its assertions, we are not only willing but anxious to delete any references to such persons in *Freedom's Frontier* or any other of our publications.' In the absence of documentation of the charges from the Texans for America, Lyons and Carnahan's willingness to delete names they had once considered worthy of inclusion raises a question as to their interest in defending *Freedom's Frontier.* The names need not be deleted unless the committee finds more adequate evidence to indicate the necessity for such deletions."

The staff of the Texas Commissioner of Education, also reporting on *Freedom's Frontier,* commented: "The publisher's representatives asked if we objected to deleting references to four names considered 'controversial.' We said in our opinion they could delete any names they wished." The records did not identify these "controversial" names.

The committee document called for the omission of "all references to and works by Pete Seeger and Langston Hughes" in Texas school books because of their recorded connections with groups cited by the House Un-American Activities Committee.

Ginn and Company got word to drop any mention of Vera Micheles Dean from its *American History:* "Dean, Vera M. – Subject is on a list of persons who are extremely well-listed as to their Communist and Communist-front affiliations by various government investigating committees."

Laidlaw Brothers eliminated from the bibliography of

Our United States the names of Marion Bauer, Ann Sterne and Dorothy Canfield Fisher.

The committee told the Macmillan Company that its *History of a Free People* needed to take a "more positive stand . . . against communism and socialism." As an example of its failure, the committee cited the following passage, which the publisher then promptly discarded: "Had Wilson seen the necessity for compromise, the United States would have joined the League, although with reservations. Had that happened, there was just a chance that World War II might have been averted."

Similarly, the Silver Burdett Company made substantial modifications in a geography text, *The American Continents.* The alterations indicate how the character of a book can be transformed through censorship efforts. The changes included:

Original version: "Today, other countries help us in protecting our land against possible attack. Radar listening posts . . ."
Changed to: "With radar we can quickly detect the approach of enemy aircraft or missiles. But radar stations . . ."

Original version: "Because it needs to trade, and because it needs military help, the United States needs the friendship of countries throughout the world. But, to keep its friends, a country must help them, too."
Changed to: "The United States trades with countries in all parts of the world. We are also providing military help to many nations. In addition, the United States aids many countries in other ways."

Original version:
"*Getting Along with One Another.* It is often hard for people of different countries to understand each other. They come from different backgrounds. They eat different foods, wear different clothes, speak different languages. The United States sometimes

finds it difficult to agree with its neighbors in all things. Nor do other countries always agree with us."

Changed to:

"*Different Ways of Living.* It is often hard for people of different countries to understand each other. They come from different backgrounds, wear different clothes, speak different languages. The people of some nations have forms of government different from ours. Often they do not enjoy the same freedom and opporunity as our people."

Original version: "When these differences arise, we Americans often become impatient. It is often hard for us to see that other countries must think first of themselves and their own welfare, just as we do of ours. We are proud of our independence. So are they. Perhaps we should always keep in mind that only seven out of every one hundred people in the world live in the United States. And these seven should not expect to tell all of the remaining ninety-three what to do.

"So, it may take a long time to reach complete understanding between our country and others. It often takes years to decide even small matters. But we must keep on trying to find agreement for the good of all. This is one important reason why the United States takes part in the United Nations. There, almost a hundred nations meet to talk about their problems. Only when all nations learn to work together in solving their problems can we be sure of lasting peace in the world."

Changed to: "Many Americans find it necessary to understand the ways in which other people live. For example, a manufacturer who does business in India must follow business practices that are often different from those of the United States. Government officials who go to other lands must also understand the differences between those lands and our own.

"Every day we read or hear of events in distant places that are of importance to the American people. To understand such events properly, we all should have some knowledge of the ways people live in those lands.

"Membership in the United Nations brings the United States into contact with almost one hundred foreign nations. The representatives of all these nations meet together at the United Nations headquarters in New York City to discuss international problems. The United States government, through its representatives, has taken a leading part in the activities in the United Nations."

By making the alterations, the publishing companies won the state textbook committee's permission to sell their books in Texas, but this did not end their sales problems. They found many local school officials unwilling to buy a book that had been under attack – even after "objectionable" sections had been stricken. D. C. Heath and Company, for example, said that the sales volume for their high-school history ran $80,000 below what sales records led them to anticipate.

Like many textbook battles, those in Texas spilled over into school libraries, and caused the banning of numerous volumes even from library shelves. The controversies revolved mostly around charges of obscenities, although the Texans and others flayed some of the library books because of their political ideas or because the authors had once belonged to groups cited by the House Un-American Activities Committee.

Ten novels, including four Pulitzer Prizewinners, were withdrawn from libraries at the four Amarillo high schools and at Amarillo College. They were *Andersonville* by MacKinlay Kantor, *Brave New World* by Aldous Huxley, *Marjorie Morningstar* by Herman Wouk, *The Big Sky* and *The Way West,* both by A. B. Guthrie, Jr., *Grapes of Wrath* by John Steinbeck and *Viking Portable Library* with selections of John Steinbeck, *Laughing Boy* by Oliver LaFarge, *1984* by George Orwell, and *Of Time and the River* by Thomas Wolfe.

Some of the same volumes had been removed earlier from school libraries at Midland where Harold H. Hitt, chairman of the State Textbook Committee, is superintendent of schools. The Texans for America circulated a pamphlet saying forty-two books at the Midland High School Library had been examined at random and the ten listed above had been analyzed as "totally unfit for consumption at any age level."

The textbook battles also sparked a legislative investigation that continued through 1962 and threatened ultimately to add to the record of censorship in the Lone Star State.

8

Glowing and Throbbing History

THE STATE of Texas, through its House of Representatives, went on record in 1961 as desiring "that the American history courses in the public schools emphasize in the textbooks our glowing and throbbing history of hearts and souls inspired by wonderful American principles and traditions. . . ."

That was part of a resolution the House adopted setting up a five-man committee to investigate the content of school books, a measure introduced by Representative Bob Bass of De Kalb at the instigation of Mrs. Forrester, the DAR-Texan book censor. Soon after the inquiry began in 1962, Bass, who was elected the vice-chairman of the committee, said he was finding the problem of subversion "much more serious than I anticipated."

The committee's hearings proved as wild as a Texas rodeo. Large crowds dominated by foot-stomping censors gave lusty applause to their witnesses and raucous boos to the opposition. They worked themselves into a frenzy when Haley and their other heroes took the stand. Some witnesses brought armloads of books with them, others carried them in suitcases. At times the hearings went on long into the night as testimony on subversion in Texas books piled up at an almost incredible rate. In this carnival-like atmosphere two committee members who consistently opposed the censorship groups were insulted by witnesses without reprimand by the chairman. One witness accused a committeeman of being a card-carrying Communist, and at a later session the chairman himself brought up the accusation without saying whether he believed it. His remark was wildly applauded by a boisterous crowd of several hundred, mostly women.

Many ministers, some seeking out subversion but others more interested in obscenities, rallied to the censorship cause. So did a number of physicians who expressed worries that Social Security was following the Communist line, particularly if it should be expanded to include medical care for the aged. Testimony from such professional quarters gave the attacks on books an aura of prestige and authority.

The chairman of the investigating committee, which was scheduled to make its recommendations to the 1963 Texas legislature, was a dairy farmer, W. T. Dungan of McKinney. A grim-faced conservative who stands about five feet six in his cowboy boots, Dungan as a lawmaker was best known for his introduction of a bill to require every public school, college and university teacher in Texas to swear his belief in a Supreme Being. (The measure died in committee.)

Dungan gave the censors free rein to discuss a variety of other subjects – mental health, fluoridation, military indoctrination, obscenities, the socialistic trend since the turn of the century, and so on. Many of the witnesses began their testimony by saying they had read no textbooks, but "knew" just the same that pupils were being subverted. The Rev. R. D. Wade of Austin's Trinity Baptist Church, saying he was unfamiliar with schoolbooks, offered instead that he was offended by a television program on which a rabbi and an Episcopal theologian had laughed at the John Birch Society's belief that there were Communists in the White House. "I have no doubt there are Communists in the White House," he said, adding that he was too busy winning "souls for Jesus Christ" to have time to "document" his charge.

The other members of the committee were Nelson Cowles, an insurance salesman of Hallsville, who sided with Dungan and Bass on most matters, and Ronald E. Roberts, a high-school history teacher from Hillsboro, and John Alaniz, an attorney from San Antonio. Roberts and Alaniz fought the censors and contested Dungan's handling of the hearings. They accused him of allowing witnesses to ramble over a wide range of irrelevant subjects and of failing to maintain decorum. And Roberts maintained "these extremist groups that have been appearing before this special committee are far more dangerous than the Communists. These fanatical groups would actually destroy democracy because of the methods they seek to impose on our society."

At an Austin session, Mrs. Roy T. Moore, representing a group from Midland, turned up with a sheaf of excerpts from several books. Lowering her eyes and blushing as she took the stand, she said in a faltering voice, "Most of this report is obscene and filthy. I would like to have my pastor help me with this report. I don't feel like . . ." Her voice trailed off into anguished silence, and up stepped the Rev. Ralph Wright, pastor of the Corinth Baptist Church of Midland, "to do her dirty work."

As a hush fell over the packed hearing room, the minister in a booming voice read excerpts from *Andersonville,* a Pulitzer Prize winner: "Page 20. 'God damn the Yankees. God damn the Yankees. God damn the Yankees. Amen!' Ought to have left off that Amen. Page 28. 'God damn you.' Page 29. 'You Yankee bastard!' Page 31. 'God damn the Yankee who did this to me.' 'May the good God damn the Yankee who did this to me.' Page 38. 'Amos, you black son of a bitch.' 'You son of a bitch go fetch a lump of alum! Don't stand there like a g– [The clergyman choked on this one and wound up spelling it] like a g-a-w-k, God damn it – fetch.' "

On and on the pastor read without interruption until he got through "Page 185. 'Hey, go stick a weasel up your ass.' " Suddenly, from the other end of the hearing table, up jumped a rotund man shouting: "Preacher! That's enough! I'm a Baptist preacher myself, and I can't stand any more!"

Mr. Wright now turned from the committee to the audience to explain his position: "Dear people, I don't mean to be out of order. But if our children read this under the lamplight of their homes, I don't think I'm out of order reading it here." But he added no more from the *Andersonville* book, nor any of the excerpts he had from *Brave New World, 1984, The Way West, The Portable Steinbeck, The Grapes of Wrath,* or *Laughing Boy.* Instead, he turned to quoting and ridiculing the Negro poet Langston Hughes, and he ended by looking around the hearing room and saying: "I thank God for this group of people gathered here – at least for most of them. Anytime you brethren need me, I'll be with you."

When her pastor had completed the "dirty work," Mrs.

Moore took the stand and said the entire books, not just the excerpts, were "trash" and that they were put on recommended reading lists as "part of the Communist conspiracy to lower the morals of youth."

J. Evetts Haley himself, the top Texan, went through his routine of criticism on the same occasion and when he had finished, Representative John Alaniz asked: "You object to the mentioning of social classes in these books?" Haley replied he did indeed because the absence of class emphasis was "why your people and mine came to this country." Alaniz, of Mexican descent, stared deadpan at Haley for several seconds, then said bluntly: "Mr. Haley, part of my people were here already." Even the Haleyites joined in the laughter.

But there was much serious work at the hearing as well as lighter moments: Out in the audience a lady legislator, whipping up support for Haley, tried to "Wake up America!" Mrs. Myra Banfield, a stylish grandmother in her forties, was acting as Americanism Chairman of the American Legion Auxiliary in Texas as well as state representative from Rosenberg. She distributed copies of her newsletter, which urged that pressure be put on the legislature to provide funds for the committee to continue its investigation. The newsletter declared:

"In my opinion, we are afforded an extraordinary opportunity to expose, and to publicize the left-wing ideology in re: public school textbooks. The 'Voice of the People' can NOW be heard. We have a sympathetic ear of a majority of the present House Investigating Committee. This is the time to strike! 'The iron is hot!' It could be the biggest awakening in Texas and Texas could lead the nation! I URGE you to get out your paper and pen and your telephone, you are as important as a man on a battlefield with a machine gun!"

The legislature did provide the funds, and Mrs. Banfield expressed her gratitude by following the committee to its hearings and ballyhooing the Haleyites and the three committeemen she considered her allies.

At two successive sessions, the censors faced their first public opposition from educators, ministers and authors. Four faculty members of the University of Texas pleaded stirringly for unfettered reading and one of them, Roger Shattuck, professor of Romance languages, whose red beard alone shocked the Haleyites, drew gasps and hisses by denouncing the House Un-American Activities Committee. Committeemen Dungan and Bass pressed the professor on this point, but the only "good" Shattuck would say for the committee was that it had aroused public opposition to its conduct. He said the committee had never sponsored any legislation.

Shattuck also told the Texas committee that in judging history there are two traditions. "One we may call the 'tears in my eyes' tradition, represented by earlier testimony today." (The reference was to a woman who showed the committee a history text printed in 1885 which she said was ideal because "it kinda stirs your heart, which I think histories should.") The second tradition he called "the kick in the pants tradition, which looks not so much to the past as to the future. . . . The danger of the first tradition is smugness, of the second cynicism. The truth lies not between them, but comes out of a debate between them."

Dr. Benjamin F. Wright, professor of government and director of the Institute of American Studies at the university, called Haley and his Texans "men and women of little faith, people of narrow views." Knowing smiles and headshaking spread across the audience when it came out that Wright had obtained his Ph.D. at Harvard.

The Rev. Lee Freeman, associate pastor of the University Baptist Church, told the committee: "It is not the purpose of American history to inspire patriotism. We love our country, but we want to know the truth. There are many things we will be ashamed of, many things we will be proud of. We don't need a mythological history that will thrill our hearts."

He also criticized the Baptist ministers who had objected to *Andersonville:* "A book ought to be judged by its total content, what it's trying to say. There are portions of the Bible, portions of the Song of Solomon, I would not read from the pulpit, just as there are portions of these books I would not read from the pulpit." *Andersonville,* he said, would be "profitable reading" for older high-school students. Following the session, a lady Texan darkly warned him that other Baptist clergymen would be apprised of his views.

Perhaps the most impressive witness against the censors — certainly one of the most outspoken — was Haley's old friend J. Frank Dobie, and students from the University of Texas jammed the room to hear him. For the first time the censorship elements did not dominate the occasion. The students knew how strongly Dobie felt on the issue, for earlier, he had publicly called the Texans for America "one of the worst things that has happened to Texas education in my lifetime," adding: "These objectors are really objecting to the twentieth century. They seem unaware of the modern treatment of social history. They want to go back to history writing that consisted mostly of accounts of wars and heroes, and that left out the masses of people."

Dobie, his white hair falling over his forehead, shook hands with Haley and sat beside him before testifying. But somehow their close friendship, which had spanned more than thirty years, had now lost some of its glow. Dobie told a reporter later that Haley – always known as a great yarn spinner and personally rather jovial when not on an ideological tangent – seemed to have misplaced his sense of humor. Anyway, they both smiled for news photographers, and then Dobie began:

"All we're asking for is to leave freedom free to combat error. We don't any of us think wisdom will die with us. . . . A censor is a tool. Or, as Hitler called Mussolini – a utensil. Not one censor of history is respected by enlightened men of any nation. . . . Any person who imagines he has a corner on the definition or conception of Americanism and wants to suppress all conceptions to the contrary is a bigot and an enemy to the free world.

"The more censoring of textbooks, the weaker they become," he went on. "Their publishers are so compliant that most of them would print the texts in Hindu if the buyers preferred. Their aim now is to offend nobody. The result is negative – something as dull as a Ph.D. thesis in a department of education."

Of the State Textbook Committee, which had bowed to some of the censorship demands, Dobie declared: "The committee is now dominated by educationists – executives in public schools. Most of them are politically minded. Few of them read anything beyond chamber of commerce proceedings and *Reader's Digest* waterings. The textbook committee should have more educated people on it. . . ."

Dobie said, "The book burners are rising again. The Minute Women. The John Birchers. The Ku Klux Klaners. Yesterday they took ten books off the shelves in Amarillo. (I didn't read that in the local newspaper.) Tomorrow what?"

The hearing ran into a night session the day Dobie spoke, and after the supper break, when he no longer was present, Haley took the stand and vehemently denounced him. Raising his voice frequently, speaking with sarcasm and bitterness, he lashed out at the "supercilious" students in the audience "who sit there and grin." He referred to Dobie as "a member of a number of subversive orders and movements," and he called the university professors "fatheads" and "left-wingers." He accused Dobie of associating with "the authentic liars of Texas," and labeled him and other anti-censorship witnesses "long-haired, super-intellectuals, super-sophisticates." He demanded to know "where was that bunch of bleeding hearts" when the University of Texas "fired" him "for teaching the truth."

Dobie, chagrined at the outburst, later told a reporter, "We've known each other many years. I didn't think he would attack me personally." He added, "But I'll say one thing for him: If he believes something is right, he'll stand alone in the blizzard and snow and fight for it. He's sincere in believing the country is going to the dogs and can be saved only by his prescription. But I don't put him on a pedestal. He is a mean fighter and will kick you where it hurts. He believes the ends justify the means. He hates, hates, hates."

Representatives Dungan and Bass, who had praised Haley and other supporters of censorship and book-banning, had little to say when they heard Dobie and four of his colleagues from the Texas Institute of Letters make their plea for freedom to read. But Bass did release a statement to the press saying Dobie appeared before the committee "with a group of characters – possibly all university students – ready to laugh and clap at the signal of Mr. Dobie. There were among the laughing and clapping group weird lookers with sideburns, some with hair so far down in their eyes they could not see – beatniks. It appeared that J. Frank Dobie appeared only to discredit the committee in the hope of killing it and leaving our textbooks and library books with the slanted outlook and vulgar phrases that they now have. There is one thing that we can be thankful for, that we have only one J. Frank Dobie and hope his kind do not multiply faster than the Good American people can keep them in control."

Amarillo was running a high censorship fever when the committee moved into west Texas to hold a hearing there. It had not been long since ten books had been taken from the school and college library shelves, a move the Amarillo *News-Globe* had lauded in a front-page editorial proclaiming its own guide for censorship: ". . . sentences too foul to print in the *News-Globe* are too foul for school libraries." Twenty-three critics showed up and had a field day; there was no opposition. Committeemen Alaniz and Roberts were insulted by witnesses who asked questions as well as testified.

When Roberts was away from the hearing room briefly, a witness, Mrs. Harold Boots, exclaimed: "Well, what happened to the gentleman from Hillsboro? I had a question for him. I wanted to ask him how long he had been a card-carrying Communist. . . ." The remark brought heavy applause from spectators and other witnesses. (Roberts, who later filed an $85,000 suit against Mrs. Boots, received a letter from Governor Price Daniel calling it a "slanderous allegation" and adding he was "shocked to learn . . . of the personal attack made against you.") Mrs. Boots, the wife of a salesman, also told Alaniz he had no business on the committee because he was a Catholic, and she charged that one sixth-grade text was "full of Catholic propaganda."

Willie Morris, editor of the *Texas Observer,* shot one of his frequent editorial barbs at the censors after Mrs. Boots' remarks: "It is a typical trick of communists, of course, to place some of their own card-carrying comrades in places of great trust, but to have imagined one on the textbook committee itself! This discovery, which could only have been made in the Panhandle, is fraught with implications. Suppose, in the committee's future peregrinations, we are to learn that a *majority* of the committee are card-carriers – a frightening prospect and a dangerous omen for our very textbooks themselves. Where will the awful truth strike next? Dungan, a special agent for Mao-Tse-Tung? Bass, a secret director of collective farms in the Ukraine? Cowles, a soulmate of Alger Hiss at Harvard? Already we have been warned, in the Amarillo hearing, that Alaniz is a Roman Catholic. It has been almost two months, and the orders may have been sent out from the Pope long ago. These are disturbing thoughts, but we may at least take solace in the knowledge that the textbook investigations have finally flowered. Where will it all end? We demand, for the safety of our commonwealth and its citizens, that the textbook committee cease investigating textbooks and start forthwith investigating itself."

Another Amarillo witness, Mrs. Gale Ledbetter, placed a small American flag in front of her when she took the stand to testify that "triumphant heroism" and "things that make America great" are needed in history books. She protested that the history of "our lovely Statue of Liberty" was not in one book and the only photograph of it was a "rear view picture."

At a San Antonio hearing, the lady censor from the Legislature, Mrs. Myra Banfield, her smile flashing on and off like a neon sign, stood near the doorway greeting the Haleyites, the Legionnaires, the Daughters and Sons of the Revolution, and other proponents of censorship. She had just welcomed one of the Daughters and turned off the smile when a reporter walked up. She turned it back on.

"Now to my way of thinking this is a very good method of evaluating books," she said, handing the reporter a pamphlet, *Elementary Textbook Evaluation Guide,* published by the National Anti-Communist League of America with headquarters in San Gabriel, California. "That's not just for books either," said the lady lawmaker. "You can use the same method to see how left-wing the press is." She was especially impressed by the first section of the pamphlet, which contained a scheme for measuring patriotism, or conversely, subversion, by tabulating the number of times certain words were used and others omitted.

Under the heading, "Words Generally Omitted (words that engender pride and individual contribution)," it listed about eighty words, including: accomplishments, achievement, admiration, bold, bravery, capacities, capitalism, challenge, character building, and conviction.

The category, "Words Often Used (words that imply control, group adjustment and class struggle)," listed about eighty more, including: adjustment, agrarian, aristocrats, attitudes, big business, bigotry, centralization, changing, clash of classes, co-exist, community and conform.

One pamphlet distributed at the hearing bore the Texans For America stamp and declared: "Some of our leading educationists have openly proclaimed their determination to change the pattern of American life. They have been alarmingly successful and few will deny that the new pattern they have traced came directly out of Marx and Lenin. We are convinced that in our vast and elaborately expensive school system, theories and ideas are propagated which are alien to our culture and destructive to our civilization."

Other literature displayed or distributed, originated in at least six states and included: a pamphlet from the Watch Washington Club, 1000 East Broad Street, Columbus, Ohio; *A Handbook for Freedom Fighters,* by Kenneth W. Ryker, Teacher Publishing Company, Dallas, Texas; *Textbook Study,* the 1958–1959 DAR report; E. Merrill Root's *Brainwashing in the High Schools;* several pamphlets from America's Future, including Rosalie Gordon's *What's Happened to Our Schools?; Rigged High School Debates Promote World Government,* a pamphlet by the *Independent American,* New Orleans; an issue of *News and Views,* publication of the Church League of America, Wheaton, Illinois, which was devoted to an article by Medford Evans entitled "Are School Textbooks Aiding in the Destruction of the American Republic?"; a copy of the monthly report of Education Information, Inc., of Fullerton, California, which contained an article on textbooks by Root; and *American History Was My Undoing* by Donzella Cross Boyle of Pro-Patria Publications, Pasadena, California, also published by Education Information, Inc.

At the request of Forrest M. Smith, Jr., a physician representing several pro-censorship witnesses, the committee opened its San Antonio session with a film entitled "The Ultimate Weapon," produced by the Volker Foundation in California. Narrated by a Hollywood actor, Ronald Reagan, it purported to show that American prisoners in Korea succumbed to brainwashing because of a "weakness in American character." Dr. Smith said the film was pertinent to upcoming testimony because "subversive" textbooks accounted for this "weakness." The movie was a short, slick production containing such catch lines by Reagan as "It beats burning bamboo splinters beneath your fingernails." This remark occurred when one of the soldiers did his captors' bidding in return for favorable treatment. But the film wound up with what seemed to be the whole point of it, that the GI's actually were weakened by a socialistic trend in this country, not just in textbooks. The picture deplored "those who seek government aid" and want "guaranteed security," such as old-age and unemployment benefits.

Though the film won vigorous applause, its most dramatic contribution came when the censorship groups ran into difficulty exhibiting it. That was when the sound failed, and a middle-aged bottle-blonde, wearing a skin-tight green dress and gold high heels, rushed from the front row to the press table and told reporters: "They've cut the wires! Sabotage! Sabotage!" Across the room the whispers rippled, "Sabotage! Somebody cut the wires! Sabotage! Sabotage!" Several censors gathered around their projector and in a moment located a technical fault which they quickly corrected.

Dr. Smith, who told newsmen that many physicians were among the thousand persons who had petitioned that the

San Antonio hearing be held, advised the committee that "the time to act is now." He said that textbooks were "maligning national heroes" and lacked "the stirring words of the Men of Seventy-Six."

Another physician, Karl M. Aijian, an immigrant from Armenia, said he opposed the "coercive features" of Social Security, farm crop controls and the National Labor Relations Board. And he further suggested that the Post Office should be operated by private enterprise.

The witnesses unquestionably had done their homework. They read lengthy prepared statements, most of which included excerpts from the propaganda of such organizations as America's Future and the DAR.

Committeeman Roberts did not stay around for the second and final day of the San Antonio hearing, and his absence again was marked by an inference as to his loyalty. When Representative John Alaniz commented that the committee had spent a lot of time looking for Communists without finding any, Chairman Dungan dumbfounded him by retorting, "Some people seem to think we have one on the committee, Mr. Alaniz." Finally, as if the young attorney could not believe what he had heard, he asked the chairman to repeat it, and Dungan did. Alaniz then asked if his remark meant he agreed with the witness who had called Roberts a card-carrying Communist. "I didn't say I agreed," said the chairman. But neither did he say he disagreed.

The audience applauded Dungan, but it erupted into catcalls and shouts of "No, no," when an anti-censorship witness denounced extremists. Maury Maverick, Jr., a former legislator whose father had been a New Deal Congressman, irritated the crowd immediately by saying he defended the memory of Franklin D. Roosevelt and the good name of

John Alaniz. His deep, resonant voice rising above the shouts from the audience, Maverick, state Democratic Committeeman, deplored the "atmosphere of fear" generated at the hearings and asserted that teachers were not testifying because they had been "intimidated and kicked around" by the extremists. He said book-burners were the same people who hated the National Council of Churches, Negroes and Jews and "they just can't wait to impeach Earl Warren and by God I stand up for that great American!" This was nothing short of heresy as far as the censors were concerned – some of them had even favored "lynching" the Chief Justice – and their boos turned to gasps.

They also had derisive shouts for H. S. Brown, president of the Texas state AFL–CIO, who criticized the Texas Education Agency for keeping incomplete records on alterations in textbooks and the publishers for making them. "Without a complete record," Brown said, "the public has no way of knowing what injustices were done by the textbook committee and by panicky publishers who feared that unless they made every change requested, plus suggesting some changes of the same type themselves, they might lose a sale."

The Texas society of the DAR formally commended the committee and affirmed that its hearings had "disclosed an alarming infiltration of subversive authors and theories" and had uncovered "slanted" books which were designed to "turn pupils away from love of God, Home and Country." The American Legion and Sons of the American Revolution in Texas also praised the committee.

Obviously pleased with the support of these groups and the Texans for America and other organizations, Chairman Dungan told a reporter in April, 1962:

"We're going to take some action all right to get the

socialist influence out of textbooks in Texas. Two of our committee members are extremely liberal and oppose our work, but they didn't see fit to resign. The rest of us feel like a lot of these complaints are justified. Some things have been purposely omitted from books and some purposely added and the socialist influence is obvious."

The committee was scheduled to make its report to the 1963 Legislature convening in January. The outlook was that it would recommend changes in adoption procedures to assure Texas schools of books that emphasize "our glowing and throbbing history of hearts and souls inspired by wonderful American principles and traditions. . . ."

9

Swing the Shining Sickle

In February, 1962, sponsored by the Rev. Billy James Hargis's Christian Crusade, the first annual "National Anti-Communist Leadership School" was held at the Mayo Hotel in Tulsa, Oklahoma. In some respects it looked like another book battle in Texas.

The Baptist minister from Midland was on hand passing out mimeographed excerpts from *Andersonville* ("God damn the Yankees. God damn the Yankees . . .") "Reverend Wright's Instant Obscenity," reporters called it.

As members of the school's "faculty," Mrs. Harry Artz Alexander of the Mississippi DAR, who had fought for censorship in Texas after leading the battle in her own state, and Meyers G. Lowman, the Circuit Rider from Cincinnati, who participated in the Texas fight, lectured on subversion in texts and education.

The one hundred seventy-eight persons who paid one hundred dollars each to attend the school also viewed the film which had touched off whispers of "sabotage" in San Antonio – "The Ultimate Weapon." And they returned to the twenty-five states from which they came with a message from Mrs. Alexander to check the textbooks in their schools and exert pressure to root out any "subversion."

The Tulsa leadership school, in its printed program, billed Mrs. Alexander as a "dynamic leader in eliminating Communist-authored textbooks from Mississippi schools" and Lowman as "publisher of public records of Communist infiltration and subversion of churches, church-related groups and educators." All faculty members were hailed as "some of America's foremost anti-Communist leaders."

Hargis said he chose his faculty carefully, to be sure there were no extremists among them. He told a reporter, "The nuts are a burden to me. They are my heartache."

On the faculty were at least six members of the John Birch Society's Committee of Endorsers and one member of its National Council. On the Christian Crusade's Board of Advisors and Endorsers in 1962 were four members of the Society's National Council and seven members of the Committee.

One of the Birchites, Dr. Revilo P. Oliver, professor of classics at the University of Illinois, told those attending the school that liberal intellectuals were "witch doctors and fakers with a sanctified itch to save the world" and were causing federal taxes to be raised for the benefit of "every mangy cannibal in Africa."

Another faculty member, R. Carter Pittman, a segregationist attorney from Dalton, Georgia, and a member of the Birch Society's Committee of Endorsers, attacked the Negro race as being biologically and intellectually inferior to the Caucasian and said the principal difference between the Negroes here and those in the Congo was that "in the Congo they eat more people than they do in the United States."

Hargis, who has a degree from Burton College and Seminary in Colorado, which was labeled by the U. S. Department of Health, Education and Welfare as a "degree mill" dealing in mail-order diplomas, is better known for his charges of Communism in the churches than for his attacks on schoolbooks. But like most Americans who carve out a career writing and talking about — and promoting a propaganda campaign against — the Communist threat as a domestic problem, he detects subversion in all corners of society. He believes a Communist take-over of this country is imminent, he says, unless he and other patriots can arouse the people to the danger before it is too late.

The *Saturday Evening Post* of April 28, 1962, said Hargis "leads his million-dollar witch-hunt in hot pursuit of the Communists he sees lurking everywhere." And the National Council of the Churches of Christ, where Hargis sees some of the Reds lurking, referred to him as a "promoter of discord and hate." But Hargis shrugs off such charges as being inevitable for anyone who has the courage to fight the Communist menace. He tells his avid followers that attacks on him are inspired by Moscow and only prove that the Christian Crusade is hurting the Communists.

Meyers Lowman, who lectured in Tulsa on two subjects — "Communist infiltration of American churches" and "transmission of pro-Communist propaganda via channels of education in America" — is a public relations man. He organized the Circuit Riders in 1951 to "oppose socialism and communism in our [Methodist] church."

Lowman has published several pamphlets to "prove" that Protestant clergymen are Communist sympathizers. The titles indicate the numbers of ministers he believes to be Communists or sympathizers: *1411 Protestant Episcopal*

Rectors, 614 Presbyterian Church, U. S. A. Clergymen, and *2109 Methodist Ministers.* He has written similar pamphlets to "prove" that many educators had Communist ties. His charges are based on membership in any organization which was ever alleged to have had a Communist taint. Much of his information dates back many years, some to World War II when Russia was an ally of the United States and many patriotic Americans were joining organizations which were friendly to the Soviet Union.

In 1954 Lowman did six months' "undercover work" for the Georgia Commission on Education, a state agency established to fight integration. His role as a "secret investigator" came to light when the Atlanta *Journal-Constitution* reported that a state audit showed he had been paid a fee of $4500. Governor Marvin Griffin subsequently issued a statement saying Lowman was recommended by "segregation leaders in Louisiana and did an excellent job for us."

Christian Crusade took in more than a million tax-exempt dollars in 1961, making it, according to the *Saturday Evening Post,* "the best-heeled of all the far-right organizations." While it may be the best financed, it is by no means the only fundamentalist religious group to encompass textbooks in the anti-Communist crusade. Included among other groups are:

—The American Council of Christian Churches, which was founded by the Rev. Carl McIntire of Collingswood, New Jersey, after he was deposed from the Presbyterian ministry in 1936 for acts of "defiance" and causing "dissension and strife." Fourteen small fundamentalist denominations with a total membership of about 300,000 are affiliated with the Council.

—The Church League of America in Wheaton, Illinois,

headed by Edgar C. Bundy, author of *Collectivism in the Churches* and a protégé of McIntire. The League's publication, *News & Views,* has carried articles by members of the John Birch Society and others attacking textbooks. Bundy boasts that he possesses "five tons of files" consisting of books, pamphlets and other propaganda published and distributed by left-wing organizations. An Air Force Reserve major who likes to be billed as "Major Bundy," he speaks frequently on Communism and conducts "counter-subversive" seminars. He led the Legionnaires in Illinois who condemned the *Girl Scout Handbook* as "un-American."

— The American Council of Christian Laymen, organized by Allen Zoll's old associate in textbook battles, Verne P. Kaub, of Madison, Wisconsin.

Of all the organizations seeking changes in textbooks, probably none has gained so much attention as the John Birch Society. What the society has tried to do in education, however, has received only minor attention from the press, which has trained the spotlight mainly on the general political and economic charges of its founder, Robert H. W. Welch, Jr.

Welch, a retired candy manufacturer from Belmont, Massachusetts, organized the secret society in December, 1958, in Indianapolis, Indiana, where he met with eleven others to outline an organized campaign of propaganda and "counter-subversion" to save the country from the internal threat of Communism. U. S. Representative Edward W. Hiestand, a California Republican and member of the Society, told the House Rules Committee in 1961 that the membership totaled about sixty thousand. By 1962 the Society had chapters in at least thirty-four states and an even larger estimated membership.

Welch is best known for his charges that many leading Americans are Communists. In a volume entitled *The Politician,* Welch wrote that President Eisenhower's brother Milton, president of Johns Hopkins University, was "actually Dwight Eisenhower's superior and boss within the Communist Party." Of the President himself Welch wrote that "there is only one possible word to describe his purposes and his actions. That word is 'treason.' " Welch distributed copies of the volume to top leaders in the Birch Society.

United States Senator Stephen Young of North Dakota introduced into the *Congressional Record* thirteen pages from *The Politician* dealing primarily with the accusations of Communism against President Eisenhower and other national leaders. "Many people are not aware of the vicious charges he makes in the book," Young said. "I think for that reason, they should become public knowledge." He said he hesitated to "give further publicity to this dastardly attack. It is unbelievable that any sane person would make such accusations against President Eisenhower. . . . The only reason why I am reluctantly giving publicity to the vicious charges made by the leaders of this society is that I believe it will serve to give needed information to people in my state and elsewhere who may be influenced by the organization."

Welch contended he did not mind the adverse publicity. In the John Birch Society *Bulletin* he wrote: "Now when Ralph McGill and Inez Robb and Eric Sevareid and Drew Pearson and Tom Storke attack us, they all have newspaper space to make that attack known, and we get the benefit at once. And if the vicious—though typically uninformed and half-baked—enmity of Ralph McGill and The Atlanta *Constitution* is not worth one new chapter a week to us in the state of Georgia, then the good citizens of that state have gone more soft, or have really been more brainwashed, than we believe to be the case."

Despite the publicity, the Society did seem to prosper, and Welch told newsmen: "We're doing a lot of work in school texts. Most of them are loaded and there aren't any decent substitutes. We need anti-Communist texts. In many cases we check with local school committees. We're getting our people elected to school committees. We're pointing out bad books and getting good elementary texts written and keeping them objective. We're not trying to do an anti-Communist job in this field, except in history. History should be American, patriotic history."

In his magazine, *American Opinion,* Welch advised his followers: "Join your local PTA at the beginning of the school year, get your conservative friends to do likewise, and go to work to take it over. You will run into real battles against determined leftists who have had everything their way. But it is time we went on the offensive to make such groups the instrument of conservative purpose. . . ." After getting the PTA groups "straightened out," Welch wrote, the Birchites should "move up the ladder as soon as you can to assert a wider influence. And don't let the dirty tactics of the opposition get you down."

One of Welch's pet projects is a "movement to impeach" Chief Justice Earl Warren. "If we could get one million Americans to read Rosalie Gordon's *Nine Men Against America,* or to learn in any other way of the facts and the significance of the worst dozen decisions of the Warren

Court," he wrote, "Warren's impeachment by the House would follow as surely and as swiftly as children dash for an open box of candy."

Although the Birch Society does not have its own textbook-reviewing apparatus, it distributes anti-textbook propaganda from America's Future and other organizations and promotes a list of "approved books," many of which were written by long-time critics of texts. A recent list included twenty-four books whose authors are connected with America's Future. The Society also promotes a list of "approved publications," practically all of which have attacked school books.

In Twin Lakes, Wisconsin, thirty miles south of Milwaukee, the conservatives literally went back to the nineteenth century for textbooks.

After the Lakewood school board voted to introduce the 1879 McGuffey Readers into the elementary-school curriculum in 1962, state officials warned that use of the books for other than supplemental reading might cost Lakeland ten thousand dollars in state aid.

Among those supporting the use of the readers was a Chicago financier, the founder of Independence Hall Association, who offered to reimburse the school if it lost the state funds. He was applauded lustily at a rally in Twin Lakes, according to the *Christian Science Monitor,* when he advocated a return to "old fashioned patriotism" and suggested that the United States ought to "deliver the first blow," instead of worrying about being the recipient of a nuclear bomb.

The Racine *Journal-Times* castigated the conservatives in an editorial: "The attempt to foist the McGuffey Readers on Wisconsin school children is not objectionable for homely virtues which the old books teach, nor for their phonetic methods, but because they are being used to promulgate a political philosophy of the far right, which is just as objectionable . . . as it would be if school textbooks were used as an opening wedge for the propaganda of the far left. Our schools are no places for anyone's political preachment or radical philosophies."

When the school board persisted in using the readers, which were first published in 1836 by William Holmes McGuffey, the parents of two Lakewood students filed a taxpayer's petition to oust four of the board members for alleged inefficiency and neglect of duty.

Six Lakewood teachers testified in behalf of the petition, and later one of them, Mrs. Doris Bannister, told reporters she and the other five had been fired. Officials confirmed the teachers were leaving the school, but said it had no connection with the controversy. "The board members were very careful to tell us that our testifying had nothing to do with our being fired," Mrs. Bannister said, and added, "This was a revelation to me. If it didn't have anything to do with our testifying, how come they kept mentioning it?"

A circuit judge later dismissed the petition with the following comment: "It has become evident to me that these four men against whom charges have been preferred were filled with the zeal of a crusader to bring about a change in the educational program of their school and for what they sincerely believe is for the betterment of the children of that community."

In Florida three women who criticized schoolbooks as subversive were hired by the legislature's Interim Committee on Education to review Florida texts. The women, members of the Palm Beach County Coalition of Patriotic Societies, an affiliate of the Florida and American coalitions, found only four of forty-three books they examined as "suitable academically as well as ideologically." They objected to such things as Benjamin Franklin being presented as a "citizen of the world" and deplored accounts of class struggles, especially when accompanied by such chapter headings as "The Poor Tenant Farmers" and "How Other People Live."

Their evaluations were presented to the committee while the Legislature was debating what newspapers called a "book burning bill." The measure was introduced by a lawmaker who had vainly tried to get the legislature to prohibit fluoridation of water and to memorialize Congress to repeal the income tax. His bill would have banned from Florida textbooks or other volumes written by Communists, persons who had invoked the Fifth Amendment when asked questions about subversive connections, or any persons who had ever been a member of an organization listed as subversive by any congressional or state legislative committee or that presented any ideology "as superior to the American system of constitutional government, American citizenship and free enterprise."

The state superintendent of schools labeled the bill "dangerous" and said, "We cannot afford to close our children's minds to the facts of our present day problems for if we do so, we shall breed mental pygmies from physical giants." He said, "There will always be extremists on any subject of a controversial nature. It is extremely dangerous, however, to take the cause of any group of people holding extreme views as seriously as they sometimes take themselves."

The legislature rejected the bill, but after a bitter fight it did pass a milder measure which added three laymen to the textbook selection committee (previously all members were teachers) and expressed the legislative intent as being opposed to the selection of texts which present any political ideology as preferable to the American system of constitutional government.

In 1961, two years after the legislative battle, patriotic groups were more successful in forcing changes in textbooks in Florida. After the president of the Lay Citizens Committee and the state chapter of the Sons of the American Revolution protested that some texts contained subversive passages, the state school superintendent replied that the selection committee had "screened them very carefully for the very sort of material to which he objects." The commission, the superintendent told newsmen, "made a number of recommendations to the publishers for deletions of some phrases that might have been considered objectionable. The publishers are making the changes."

The Los Angeles *Herald and Express* (now the *Herald-Examiner*) was furious. One of its reporters had examined textbooks for subversive content and had found, among other things, that a music book contained a "ditty from behind the Iron Curtain."

A headline in the Hearst newspaper reported: " 'God Bless America' Is Replaced by 'Shining Sickle' Song." "A flagrant slap at patriotism," cried the *Herald and Express* in telling how it had spotted "Swing the Shining Sickle" in a book up for adoption in California.

The truth was that the song was composed in 1897 as an American harvest song relating to Thanksgiving.

The *Herald and Express,* in a series of articles designed to whip up opposition to the adoption of thirteen books for fifth- and eighth-graders, hurled many other charges of subversion. One author was accused of taking "a rather blithe view of American history" because his text contained only two pictures of the American flag and devoted only one paragraph to "Washington and his comrades." The newspaper put "comrades" in capital letters and commented that it was a "key word in designating members of the Soviet Communist Party."

The newspaper complained that several of the authors were deficient in the number of times they used such words as "liberty," "freedom," and "republic."

The apprehension of the *Herald and Express* extended throughout the California school system, which it reported "is being successfully exploited by the Communist conspiracy. Its devious tentacles are slowly taking a stranglehold on our youth. To further ignore the spectre of this strangulation would be sheer folly." One article began this way:

"On any given day during the scholastic year, the school-age sons and daughters of California are slowly being molded into a faceless group of young non-entities who, in time, can be dangled like little puppets on the string of communism. They are being molded into a collective force to eventually tip the scales in communism's relentless struggle to dominate the world."

The newspaper did what reporters would call a "hatchet job" on the state Department of Education. It cited this passage from a department bulletin: "The goals of education are concerned directly with student attitudes. Because much of behavior is determined by the attitudes held, the logical first step in furthering certain school objectives should be to develop those attitudes in students which will result in the kinds of behavior desired. . . ." The *Herald and Express* analyzed this for its readers as "a tacit admission that education's role today is no longer that of teaching subjects, but of creating a change in attitude and behavior of school children." And then it brought down the hatchet: "What more could the Communists ask for than a change which advocates a lessening of our heritage in the public schools? It is a change which they, too, are advocating in a conspiracy to topple American democracy. . . ."

Citing a reference to "social controls" in a report by the department's Central Committee on Social Studies, the newspaper declared: " 'Social controls' is the very heart of the Communist conspiracy, the cornerstone from which it has leaped to domination over literally millions of people who were at one time free."

Again referring to the report from "this 'central committee,' " it objected to this passage: "All nations of the modern world are part of a global interdependent system of economic, social, cultural and political life." Said the *Herald and Express:* "If this doesn't fit into the hip pocket of Khrushchev's scheme of things, he missed his lessons from Lenin."

The newspaper accused the State Board of Education of an "almost overt effort to 'de-emphasize' our American heritage in California schools. In most cases, the state board is aided and abetted by local school districts and boards of education in its mad rush to eliminate all of the nation's inherited loyalties, truths and values. One need not conjecture too long that this program of playing down America is meeting with the utmost approval by the communists—if not their most forthright direction."

Roy E. Simpson, state Superintendent of Public Instruction, accused the *Herald and Express* of "distortions" and "outright falsifications" and said its series was "the best ally of communism, for it focuses unwarranted suspicion on our schools and the students in them. Communism thrives on confusion and distrust." The president of the Board of Education referred to the criticism as "poppycock."

But the newspaper stimulated considerable support for its crusade, too, and several groups began working together to protest the adoption of the books it had attacked. The San Francisco *Chronicle* noted in an editorial: "A number of busybody committees in Los Angeles are on the warpath against a batch of . . . textbooks now up for adoptions," and it said one of the groups, Parents for Better Education, actually was "Parents for Birchist Education."

The PBE, as it was called by the press, joined with such censorship groups as the National Anti-Communist League of San Gabriel and the Liberty Torch Bearers of San Fernando Valley in a concerted drive against favorable mention of the United Nations and other irritants of the ultra-conservatives.

As the groups flooded the board of education with protests, the San Francisco *News-Call Bulletin* reported that one publisher had dropped an entire chapter on the United Nations. "To make up in part for the omission of the UN chapter," the newspaper reported, the publisher added "a section drawn from the American Legion manual, on display of the flag." Educators expressed surprise at the deletion and the Americans for Democratic Action called it an "appalling" concession to the "radical right." The publisher denied he had been influenced by pressure groups.

When the board met in February, 1962, to adopt the books, an audience of four hundred gathered, most of them to cheer for the censors. The woman who heads the Liberty Torch Bearers presented a petition with six hundred signatures opposing adoption. Walter A. Wolford, president of the National Anti-Communist League and city clerk of San Gabriel, attacked the books as subversive. Under questioning, he acknowledged that the one hundred members of his "national" organization lived in California, but he said the league's "information services" had been used in states as far away as Connecticut. Representatives of the Keep America Committee, the PBE, and the West Coast Conservatives League also spoke against adoption.

There was forceful support for the books, too, led by Dr. Robert A. Skaife, representing ten thousand teachers as head of the Affiliated Teacher Organizations of Los Angeles. Dr. Skaife, who formerly headed the NEA's anti-censorship program, declared: "Boiled down, these criticisms follow a pattern which began after World War II when a trend away from New Deal principles began. Statements which in any way could be twisted by interpretation into favorable disposition of such topics as TVA, socialized medicine, FEPC legislation, the UN and UNESCO were seized upon by critics as evidence that a book under consideration was slanted toward collectivism and Communism."

Dr. Skaife called the *Herald and Express* articles "an attempt to use the schools as a means for furthering the political views of one segment of our population." He said, "The noise and furor raised over the books under consideration for adoption represents a slap at the teaching profession. In effect critics are saying that professionally trained teachers are not competent to select good teaching tools."

The board seemed unimpressed by the censorship groups and generally stood firm. But it did recommend several changes. It advised one publisher to rewrite a seven-page section of one book to indicate "that certain functions can best be left to individuals or locally controlled agencies or organizations rather than relying on governmental agencies to perform all functions."

Another publisher was told to use the term "Allies" instead of "United Nations" when referring to the countries which fought with the United States during World War II. The board suggested this insertion to clarify the matter: "Early in January, 1942, all the nations fighting against the Axis signed a statement declaring they would be known jointly as the United Nations. (This term as used then is not to be confused with the organization set up in 1945 and at that time called the United Nations Organization.) However, the nations with which the United States fought were often referred to as the Allied powers or the Allies. To avoid confusion, they are so called in this book."

That the clamor against textbooks in California has been constant is not surprising in view of an NEA report which identified the state as the major source of propaganda against the nation's public schools.

California is a favorite stamping ground for the DAR, the John Birch Society and the Circuit Riders, and is a breeding ground for such groups as the Minutemen, the Minute Women, Pro America, For America, Education Information, Inc., the Institute for Special Research, Educational News Service, and other organizations which attack public education and textbooks.

10

Other Voices

IN THE FALL of 1960, Nancy Jacobs, one of ten Negroes among the seventeen hundred students at the public high school in Torrington, Connecticut, thumbed through one of her English texts. A passage, from Joel Chandler Harris's "A French Tar-Baby" caught her eye. "When the doll was finished," the passage read, "he spread tar on it here and there . . . until it was as black as a Guinea negro."

Nancy was "disturbed" by the reference to her race, and her indignation grew as she scanned the remaining pages of *Short Stories for English Courses,* a volume published by Scribner. She found that Edgar Allan Poe's *The Gold Bug* uses the word "nigger." She was also offended by *Sonny's Christening,* an account of Arkansas country life by Ruth Stuart.

When Nancy's father, Frank Jacobs, the president of the Litchfield County branch of the National Association for the Advancement of Colored People, came home that day from his job as a machinist, Nancy showed him the book. Jacobs went to see School Superintendent John D. Hogan, and followed up his visit with a formal complaint from his NAACP branch.

Nancy's anthology, said the branch, contained "humiliating and derogatory references to the Negro" and "places the Negro in a rather unfavorable light with the obvious intent to make him appear as an inferior person."

Superintendent Hogan did not agree. "I just don't know where this sort of thing stops," he told Jacobs and other NAACP members. "There are references in all types of literature to national and occupational groups which somebody, somewhere, might take exception to." But Hogan took up the matter with the school board. Members of the board read the anthology and said that neither the school nor the books in it advocated racial discrimination. "Book burning and misguided censorship," it added, is not the way to achieve a proper education for any child. Eventually, however, the board announced that it was replacing its one hundred and sixty volumes of the text – at the rate of thirty to fifty copies a year – with a later edition of the same book – an edition which did not contain the controversial stories.

While censorship campaigns of the type waged in Torrington happen less frequently and are far less concerted than those emanating from right-wing groups, they have, nevertheless, over the years also influenced publishers in deciding what type of literature to put before the school child. Not only the NAACP, but the Anti-Defamation League of B'nai B'rith, and, on occasion, other crusading or religious organizations screen textbooks for matter they consider objectionable.

A section in the NAACP constitution directs each local branch to "familiarize itself with material used in the schools and seek to eliminate material therefrom which is racially derogatory." The provision was supplemented in

1961 by a resolution of the fifty-second annual convention of the NAACP, urging the branches "to survey textbooks in use in their community schools for the purpose of ensuring that textbooks and other educational material properly present the contribution of the Negro to American culture."

The national office distributes copies of the constitution and resolutions to the local branches, but otherwise does not push for screening campaigns. "Anything done about textbooks today is done on the local level," says Gloster Current, the NAACP's director of branches. "There hasn't been a consistent textbook drive from the national office since more than twenty years ago when the late Charles Edward Russell made school literature a major project."

In the thirties and forties, when Russell was active, school songbooks – particularly those with songs by Stephen Foster – were frequent targets. NAACP members objected to the word "darkie" in Foster's songs and eventually succeeded in having it removed from almost every songbook. In 1958 the supervisor of music for the Washington, D.C., school system told a reporter that selection committees in the District of Columbia had long refused to approve volumes containing Foster's original lyrics. Publishers had changed many of the words, he said, to make their books eligible for purchase in Washington and in other school systems with such strictures. Foster's famous line, "Oh, darkies how my heart grows weary" now reads "Oh, old folks . . ." in some books and "Oh, brother . . ." in others.

Since the forties NAACP attacks have been sporadic. A college text, *The Growth of the American Republic* by Samuel Eliot Morison and Henry Steele Commager, was assailed at the College of the City of New York by the campus chapters of the NAACP and the Young Progressives of America. The two historians, the organizations charged, gave a distorted view of the Negro during the periods of slavery and Reconstruction. The history department at CCNY refused to yield to demands to ban the book. But the volume was dropped by another New York institution, Queens College, when the NAACP chapter there cried out against it.

In reporting the censorship campaign at CCNY, *Commentary* called the Young Progressives a "fellow traveling" outfit and the NAACP a "liberal" organization. And the magazine noted that censorship can be as oppressive when waged from the political left as when it is carried on by organizations on the right.

Another censorship incident took place in New York in 1957. After receiving a complaint from a member of the Brooklyn Branch of the NAACP, the city's board of education banished Mark Twain's celebrated *Huckleberry Finn* as a reading text in elementary and junior high schools. The reason? A central character in the classic is "Miss Watson's big nigger, named Jim."

The Huck Finn case disturbed newspapers with long records of support for the Negro's struggle for equality. "The truth is," said the New York *Times,* "that *Huckleberry Finn* is one of the deadliest satires that was ever written on some of the nonsense that goes with inequality of the races.

"What happens when Huck's conscience begins to trouble him about running off with another person's slave? Huck decides that if he doesn't undo this crime by letting Miss Watson know where Jim is, he will go to hell. But then he gets to 'thinking over our trip down the river; and I see Jim before me all the time; in the day and in the night time, sometimes moonlight, sometimes storms, and we afloating along talking and singing and laughing . . . and how good he always was.' So Huck tears up the note he was going to send to Miss Watson and then says to himself 'all right, then I'll go to hell.' "

The Portland *Oregonian* also protested against the treatment of Mark Twain's classic. "The Negro has a strong case in objecting to the stereotyping of the race as comical and slow witted," the paper said. "But, in carrying the opposition to what to some may seem the logical extreme – the proscription or bowdlerizing of Mark Twain and Stephen Foster – does not the Negro thus reject his own heritage and culture, a valued part of the heritage and culture of all America? It is, in fact, a disservice to the American Negro to pretend that he always had advantages and privileges accorded most other Americans, to pretend that the Missouri slave of 1840 talked and thought as does Dr. Ralph Bunche. . . ."

While the national office of the NAACP does not participate in textbook censorship programs, neither does it oppose them. "The point of view many Negroes take is that if you can ban the use of words in *Tropic of Cancer* [the book by Henry Miller] for use in the schools, why can't you ban words like kike, nigger and darkie?" said the NAACP's Gloster Current.

"We don't like the role of censor," declared Henry Lee Moon, director of public relations for the NAACP. "But we do feel that some of the literature can be damaging to the Negro child and to the white child to the extent it gives a false impression of the Negro."

The Anti-Defamation League of B'nai B'rith, like the national office of the NAACP, has curbed its efforts to proscribe books. Until recent years it opposed the use of volumes such as the *Merchant of Venice* by Shakespeare, *Oliver Twist* by Charles Dickens, and *Little Black Sambo* by Helen Bannerman, on grounds that they promoted Jewish or Negro stereotypes. Today, however, there is within the organization a school of thought which doubts the wisdom of having books thrown out of the classroom.

"Our purpose is not to censor," says Dr. Morton J. Sobel, director of the ADL's National Department of Colleges and Universities. "Our position on books like *Oliver Twist* and *Merchant of Venice* is not to ban them but to have them taught in context and with proper explanation. We don't believe in attacking particular books as do some of the right wing groups."

While this attitude appears to be the prevailing one within the ADL, some staff members share another viewpoint. "*Little Black Sambo* and the *Gold Bug* have Negro stereotypes which just should not be used in the schools any more than you would teach a student to say 'eenie, meanie, minie, mo . . . ,' " says Miss Gertrude Noar, director of the ADL's National Education Department. "And if a teacher is anti-Semitic she can use Shylock [a major character in *Merchant of Venice*] as an excuse for passing on her prejudices to the student. There is so much literature to choose from that the school is better advised to leave such books off the approved list."

Despite Miss Noar's reservations about certain volumes, the ADL in its literature carefully avoids statements that might provoke an attack on a specific text or author. Its 1961 report, *The Treatment of Minorities in Secondary*

School Textbooks, discusses forty-eight works, but does so without name-calling. The report, for example, disapproved of a volume which dealt with the Crucifixion in these terms: "The mass of Jewish people turned against Him, and supported the priestly caste. They denounced Him to the Romans, saying that he planned to make Himself King of the Jews. He was tried as a rebel by the Roman government, condemned, and executed by Crucifixion." But the report did not give the name, title or publisher of the book which, it felt, had made it appear that "all Jews wished to have Jesus put to death."

The ADL also avoided listing the books it liked. One unidentified volume was praised by the report for saying of ancient Judaism: "Your standards of right and wrong have been developed largely from the ideals of the Hebrews and the Christians. The Ten Commandments of the Hebrew Old Testament have been written into the laws under which you live. And the ancient Christian teaching to 'love thy neighbor as thyself' expresses an ideal that is very much alive in your world. . . . [The Hebrews] believed that there is one God of the whole universe and that belief has become a part of our own culture."

The purpose of the report, the ADL has explained, was not to "pressure" publishers, and educators, but to give them the ADL's thoughts on how minorities should be treated. In spelling out their conclusions, the staff members stated that a majority of the texts "present a largely white, Protestant Anglo-Saxon view of history and the current social scene. The complex nature and problems of American minority groups are largely neglected or, in a number of cases, distorted."

The staff members further expressed alarm at the "paucity of forthright material on what Hitler did to millions of minority-group members in Germany and the lands he conquered. . . . Although no text gives sympathetic treatment to those acts, the fact remains that too few of the popular texts communicate the essential facts of Nazi atrocities to the student."

Another charge was that "the Negroes' position in contemporary American society continues to be very largely ignored. There is a tendency to treat racial inequality and attempts at its eradication with complacent generalizations, not hard facts."

The ADL was pleased, however, that none of the texts referred to the Jews as a race – a practice some books had followed in the forties. But it urged the publishers to go a step further and say, "Jews do not belong to any single race. They are usually identified by their religion."

Throughout its report the ADL followed the procedures used by the American Council on Education in its dispassionate, 1949 analysis of "intergroup relations in teaching materials." Some publishers and educators, however, privately point to "an important difference" between the two studies. The Council's analysis was compiled by educators who considered intergroup relations in the framework of broader educational goals. The ADL is an organization which operates outside the sphere of public education and whose staff members' professional interests are directed toward the goals of the ADL – not the far-reaching aims of the educational system.

The screening done by the NAACP and the Anti-Defamation League has been widely publicized. Less well known, perhaps, is the pressure exerted by Southern segregationists to keep Negro pictures out of textbooks and to limit the author's discussion of civil rights issues.

In 1955, the Georgia Board of Education banned three texts as not being "in accord with the Southern way of life." *Our Changing Social Order* by Gavian, Gray and Grove was not satisfactory, the board said, because it indicated that "white people are unfair to the Negroes in elections, in school facilities and in recreation." *America, Land of Freedom,* by Gertrude Hartman, "didn't give the South sufficient credit in the Revolutionary War." And a songbook, *Together We Sing,* was discarded because the word "darkies" in a Stephen Foster song appeared as "brothers."

In Georgia's Chatham County in 1961, a grand jury ordered school officials to clear school library shelves of several books which dealt with racial problems. Among them were: Oliver La Farge's *Laughing Boy,* a Pulitzer Prize-winning story of a young Navaho Indian couple and their conflicts with the white man's civilization; *Color Blind* by Margaret Halsey, a nonfiction work about the relationship of white and Negro soldiers during World War II; and perhaps the easiest case to understand if not to condone – *Black Boy* by Richard Wright.

Segregationists in Alabama complained during the same period because a text had included a picture of former Secretary of State Christian Herter shaking hands with the president of Nigeria.

The outcries of segregationists against "integrationist" books, however, tell only a fraction of the story in the South. Segregationists have proved most successful in influencing the content of textbooks when as members of state textbook committees they quietly refuse to buy a volume because of its pictorial content or its statements about racial equality.

Knowing that they may lose sales if their books contain Negro pictures, publishers frequently omit them — an action which led the New York City Board of Education to complain in 1959 that texts weren't giving a "factually adequate representation of the realities of social life in America today." The board said that, when Negroes are portrayed at all, they are depicted at one extreme or the other of the social scale — as cotton pickers or as celebrities.

In addition to the attacks from segregationists, minority groups, and right-wing organizations, texts occasionally draw fire from groups feuding over religious issues. In the early sixties, for example, an official of the Cincinnati chapter of Protestants and Other Americans United for the Separation of Church and State distributed a mimeographed pamphlet charging that some texts had a pro-Catholic bias. Among the reasons for the charge? A word count showed the books gave more attention to priests than to Protestant clergymen in the era in which the New World was being explored!

In the late forties, the anti-Catholic publication *The Protestant* busied itself by organizing a "Textbook Commission to Eliminate Anti-Semitic Statements in American Textbooks." The project died aborning, however, when the Anti-Defamation League and the American Jewish Committee refused any part in a campaign backed by an anti-Catholic paper. "A careful study of the files of the Protestant reveals that the periodical tends to arouse animosity and distrust among people of different creeds," said the American Jewish Committee. "We look with disfavor on any controversy between Protestant, Catholic and other religious publications or groups," the Anti-Defamation League added.

The Roman Catholics enter into the picture by frequently demanding that textbooks be especially written for their schools. Most of the major publishing firms find it necessary to put out Catholic editions of readers, histories, songbooks and even arithmetics to compete for sales in some of the parochial schools. Sometimes they feel called upon to prepare a text in more than one Catholic edition. "It is somewhat surprising to learn," said Robert Bierstedt in *Text Materials in Modern Education,* "that not all Catholic schools and colleges use the same texts in the same disciplines. Three Catholic institutions in the New York area, for example, will be found using different textbooks, because they are administered by different monastic orders within Catholicism. At the far right of Catholic philosophy we find educators insisting that a proper definition of the doctrine of original sin belongs in all courses in economics, politics, sociology, and history. . . ."

To the publisher it sometimes appears that everyone is trying to tell him how to write his books. "Every so often," says one book editor, "I look through the morning's mail and begin feeling that the only way we could escape criticism is to print a different textbook for each school child."

11

The Publisher's Dilemma

IN A CANDID MOMENT in 1960, a deputy superintendent of the school system in the District of Columbia revealed his formula for avoiding controversy over textbooks. The plan was simplicity itself. "We try to make sure that the books we select are not objectionable to anyone," Lawson J. Cantrell explained to reporters.

In the sense that it has prevented the Texas brand of textbook haranguing from spilling into the nation's capital, Cantrell's policy has worked. But such an outlook means that the *Merchant of Venice,* the *Uncle Remus* stories and *Little Black Sambo* are not used in Washington schools. The policy of super-caution led, in 1959, to the removal of a popular text, *Our Country's History* by David S. Muzzey, because it contained such historically defensible statements as: "Few of the freed slaves had any sense of responsibility. . . . They believed that the day of Jubilee had arrived and that the plantations of their former masters were to be divided among them as a Christmas gift. Every Negro would receive forty acres and a mule."

Earlier, an entire series of foreign relations booklets developed by the North Central Association of Colleges and Secondary Schools failed to win approval from District of Columbia school officials. The reason? One pamphlet contained a single sentence which could be construed as indicating a "soft attitude" toward Chinese Reds: "The communists, on the other hand, won the approval of these groups by the manner in which they governed the areas under their control."

Not all school officials state their textbook policy as clearly as Cantrell, but many of them are equally cautious, a factor that publishers cannot afford to ignore when preparing books for distributions. "How many good books do school authorities refuse to consider for adoption just because those books have been subjected to attack?" asked William E. Spaulding, the president of the Houghton Mifflin publishing house. Answering his own question, he said: "Many a superintendent of schools has quite naturally said to himself, if not to a bookman, 'I don't want a book that's been under fire. It may get me into trouble and I don't need to look for trouble these days.' "

Most publishers are, like Spaulding, well aware that an onslaught of criticism against a text by a right-wing or minority group can touch off a chain reaction among textbook selection committees and cause sales to drop in many areas. The Philadelphia school system, for example, shelved a reading program it had been using for two years after learning that the instructional material had been removed from the approved list in Ventura, California. A Ventura parent had complained that some eight or nine (out of four thousand) test questions in *Reading for Understanding* raised questions which were "detrimental to democracy." Upon re-examining the reading program, however, the Philadelphia school officials reinstated it, but not before giving the publisher, Science Research Associates, some anxious moments.

The caution of school administrators in such geographically scattered areas as the District of Columbia, California and Philadelphia leads, in turn, to timidity on the part of the publishers. The expense of producing a book is too high, many of them believe, to take chances on content which might offend potential buyers. They estimate that it costs $125,000 to write, edit, illustrate, print and bind a history text and the accompanying teachers' manuals. A firm must invest a million or more, says D. C. Heath and Company, to prepare a series of readers for grades two through six. And once the book is out it encounters stiff competition. In 1962, more than fifty publishing houses were competing for an estimated 232 million dollars in textbook business from the nation's elementary and high schools.

A cautious, competitive publishing policy means, for example, that most publishers studiously avoid the term "Civil War" for fear of offending school officials in the South. The term, "War Between the States," book salesmen have learned through years of selling experience, sounds much sweeter to Southern ears.

In the July, 1962, issue of *Harper's,* Martin Mayer says the mad scramble for sales has given the book salesman tremendous influence over the volumes his company publishes: "Every publisher knows what he *can't* sell, and will insist that such things be kept out of his satchel.

"In the obvious case," wrote Mayer, "nobody who works a Southern territory can tolerate anything that smacks of integration. Rand McNally, showing more courage than most firms, printed two versions of a social-studies text, one of them with a picture of a New York chemistry class which showed some Puerto Rican faces at the lab tables (for Northern distribution), the other with a picture of a lily-white chemistry class (for Southern distribution). Most publishers simply avoid any picture of the races together. A Macmillan civics text got into final proof with a picture of an integrated playground; a salesman spotted it and screamed; and Macmillan, with a gesture of rebuke to the editor responsible, remade the book with a different picture. Roy Peterson's American History text, complete through the 1960 election, deals with the Southern resistance to the Supreme Court in a single sentence. . . ."

Other taboos widely observed by publishing houses are almost too numerous to cite. A vice-president of McGraw-Hill says all publishers must be wary in their treatment of birth control, evolution ("some publishers use terms like organic and genetic development"), sex education and minority groups. Literature circulated by the American Textbook Publishers Institute, an organization financed by many of the leading publishing houses, shows that the taboos go still farther. In its pamphlet *Textbooks Are Indispensable,* the Institute says publishers "must try to avoid statements that might prove offensive to economic, religious, racial or social groups or any civic, fraternal, patriotic or philanthropic societies in the whole United States." Considering the multiplicity of special interest groups and the many causes they champion, this concern over "offensive" material means that publishers must weigh every word they print.

In a sense then, organizations like the Daughters of the American Revolution, America's Future, Inc., and Texans for America can achieve results simply by screaming long and loud about references to Social Security, the graduated income tax, the United Nations and the New Deal. Under the barrage of criticism such issues become "controversial"; educators in some areas hesitate to buy books which treat these matters in any detail; and publishers, fearful of losing sales, censor their own texts to bring them in line.

Anthologies of English and American literature are often affected by the same fear of controversy. Works by many widely acclaimed novelists, poets and playwrights are not found in today's texts. But perhaps publishers cannot be blamed for omitting them in view of the attitudes of many school administrators and parents. In some parts of the United States it is worth a teacher's job to put modern novels such as J. D. Salinger's *The Catcher in the Rye* or George Orwell's *1984* on a classroom reading list.

In 1960, eight angry parents stormed into the office of Charles C. Mason, superintendent of schools in Tulsa, Oklahoma, to demand that he fire a teacher who had supplied her sixteen-year-old students with paperback copies of *The Catcher in the Rye.* Superintendent Mason concluded, after reading a page which included a four-letter word, that the book was "shocking."

The teacher in question, Mrs. Beatrice Levin, herself a novelist, protested that *Catcher* was one of the most admired novels on modern college campuses. It was, she said, a "beautiful and moving" account of the "coming of age of a teenager." To the chagrin of many of her students, Mrs. Levin resigned her teaching position because school administrators had given her no backing "on my stand concerning my choice of the book."

A similar row over *The Catcher in the Rye* resulted in the dismissal, in 1960, of a Louisville, Kentucky, teacher.

In Wrenshall, Minnesota, a teacher was fired after refusing to remove *1984* from his reading list. He eventually won reinstatement, however, after arguing that the book "illustrates what happens in a totalitarian society." Other communities have banned "controversial books" but left teachers who used them in their jobs. *The Catcher in the Rye* was eliminated from supplementary reading lists in San Jose, California, along with *The Sun Also Rises* by Ernest Hemingway, *Brave New World* by Aldous Huxley, *Look Homeward, Angel* by Thomas Wolfe, and the *Human Comedy* by William Saroyan. In Miami, in 1960, both *Brave New World* and *1984* were withdrawn from a teacher's list of required reading.

After reading accounts of controversies like those in Wrenshall, Tulsa, Louisville, San Jose and Miami, publishers find it safer to fill their anthologies with works safely removed from the twentieth century, such as *Ivanhoe* and *Silas Marner*.

Many companies dislike following the taboos, but feel they can break them only at the risk of sacrificing their profits. "The mandates and taboos of regional pride, religious and political sectarianism cannot be safely ignored," P. A. Knowlton, an official of the Macmillan Company, once commented. "A picture of a hillbilly log cabin with an appropriate caption once lost one publisher a geography adoption in what later became a highly enlightened state. Thus the authors and publishers of biologies, histories, geographies, problems texts and anthologies restrain themselves here and tiptoe there. It is surprising that so much controversial material remains."

Knowlton's observations appeared in *School Executive* in 1950 and the situation today, if anything, is worse. Publishers continue to tread softly in controversial areas but pressure groups somehow still manage to find plenty in the textbooks to complain about. Thus, to silence critics and meet sales quotas, the publishers often make changes and deletions after a book appears in print.

Many of the alterations made to win business in Texas and California are, as has been seen, a matter of public record. In other states, they are made on the basis of oral agreements between publisher and textbook committee and are harder to document. Occasionally, however, a newspaper will become sufficiently interested to ferret out changes.

In its 1959 edition of *Our World Through the Ages*, Prentice-Hall, Inc., deleted a passage which said: ". . . Every race has made its contribution to world progress. This is not surprising. Scientists insist that no race is inferior to any other race in intelligence or general ability. They maintain that, where one race may appear to have made little progress, this seeming inferiority may be explained by poor environment and lack of education." To omit the passage, which had been in the book for at least five years, the publisher inserted a new page printed on a paper of different texture. William Tazewell and Luther Carter, reporters for the *Virginian-Pilot* in Norfolk, Virginia, discovered the substitution and called one of the authors to determine if it had resulted from pressure from Virginia. "All we know is that the editor called up," said Nathaniel Platt, a New York City teacher and author. "He said some people objected to it [the passage]."

Before they ended their investigation, Tazewell and Carter were wondering how regularly such changes were made. Mrs. Gladys V. Morton, chairman of the textbook committee of the Virginia Board of Education, told them: "All the publishers cooperate with the board to the extent that they do just about anything the board asks." Mrs. Morton would not go into details, however. "This business is too serious to make stories from. The less we say about changes made by the publishers the better."

The publishers are not always so secretive. Many see the matter as one of economic necessity. Deletions and rewrites, as they view them, are distasteful concessions they must sometimes make to keep their firms in sound financial condition. The regrettable fact is that changes made to appease a textbook selection committee in Mississippi, Virginia, Texas or California are frequently carried over into copies used in other states.

"There is no rule as to whether the changes made for one state will go into a book used in another state," says Homer Lucas, president of Ginn and Company, one of the larger textbook publishing houses. "But normally if the change is not objectionable it will go in all editions. If it is objectionable it will not." This immediately raises the question of just what does or does not constitute an objectionable change. The answer, of course, varies from publisher to publisher.

In early 1962, the Texas state Textbook Committee told Ginn and Company it could not market its *American History* in Texas if it did not drop Vera M. Dean's name from a list of authors suggested for supplementary reading. "Imagine objecting to Vera Dean," says Lucas. "But in a case like this, we will have to sacrifice her name in all books. It would be too expensive to make a special edition just for Texas."

How have the taboos and alterations affected the quality of textbooks?

In their book *The Freedom to Read,* authors Richard McKeon, Robert K. Merton and Robert Gellhorn charged that the tendency of publishers to comply with the demands of particular states tends "to limit what is available to other schools in other parts of the country. . . . Mississippi's views on segregation," they said, "may determine what Maine can read."

Dr. Albert Alexander, a former textbook analyst for the New York City Board of Education, contends the modern textbook is "gray flannel." In an article for *Social Education* in 1960, Dr. Alexander wrote, "a point of view by the author . . . is becoming more of a rarity as controversy is consciously avoided and the issues often artificially balanced. Too frequently the modern American history textbook has the frightful appearance of an oversized menu which attempts to please everyone by quantity and blandness." Today's school histories, Dr. Alexander is convinced, "betray a basic lack of confidence in presenting this country full face because some of the warts might show."

"The whole purpose seems to be," historian Henry Steele Commager says of textbooks, "to take out any ideas to which anybody might object and balance all sections and interests."

Another complaint comes from John B. Emerson, the chairman of the history department at Germantown Friends School in Philadelphia. He and his colleagues on the school's staff became so dissatisfied with the many "insipid" history texts that they decided to stop using them. In their place, Emerson substituted such paperbacks as *A Pocket History of the United States* by Allan Nevins and Henry

Steele Commager and *Great Issues in American History* by Richard Hofstadter. He will return to conventional texts when, and if, they become "good, sound, scholarly, readable and exciting texts, in which the author sticks his neck out in stating historical theory and challenging the student to critical thinking."

Oscar Handlin, a Harvard professor and winner of the Pulitzer Prize for history, examined several high-school texts in 1960 and found their imitativeness to be "shocking." Said Handlin: "Although some of them were by very distinguished authors, I was dismayed by the low intellectual level. It seemed to me that a good deal of responsibility must be placed among the authors themselves. . . . The unwillingness to raise questions of any sort must make the subject frightfully deadening to the student compelled to use these books."

Paul Woodring, the education editor of the *Saturday Review,* thinks that more soundly based, scholarly criticism – as opposed to the ranting of pressure groups – might bring about a change in the quality of schoolbooks. "Texts have fallen upon dull days," he says. "I think it is impossible to write a lively history without some interpretation and that entails a point of view." But, unlike some publishers and authors, he believes that texts could be interpretive without becoming "an instrument of social change" or a vehicle which would guide the student to a particular political party.

Much of the blandness could be corrected, Woodring says, if publishers and educators worried less about possible objections. "If I let criticism bother me, I would never write an article," he says. "Teachers haven't yet learned to live with criticism. A superintendent has to have courage if he is to do a good job. . . . Most of these charges against textbooks need to be viewed in perspective. Plato is un-American and yet we teach him."

Unlike the pressure groups, which often try to make it appear that everything about textbooks is bad, the scholarly critics find much in them to praise. "As a whole, they present well written and well chosen material prepared by scholars and educators," says Mark M. Krug, an education professor at the University of Chicago, in a 1960 issue of *School Review*. "Pictures, graphs, tests and documents further enhance the value of today's textbooks."

"What is needed," Krug adds, "is a balanced and responsible reappraisal of the policy of omitting or glossing over controversial issues. . . . There seems to be no valid reason why textbook writers and publishers, who have done so much to improve textbooks in the field of social studies, should not further improve them by making the books not only scholarly and attractive but also stimulating and challenging – better tools for a more effective education of the future citizens of our democracy."

Publishers are as conscious of the criticism from educators and scholars, of course, as they are of the charges from pressure groups. Some of them answer by saying that the schools are getting the kind of books they want, that books will become more provocative only when school systems are willing to face up to possible attacks from censors. Others say they are promoting "national unity" (and sales too, they might add) in publishing books that, by avoiding controversy, are acceptable in every state. Still others are convinced that they could meet the charges from scholarly critics only by allowing their authors to interpret issues as they see fit. This is an approach some publishers are reluctant to take.

A Ginn and Company editor, one who opposes "interpretive" texts, told an author of this book: "Critics on both sides want the texts to be more interpretive. But they want only their interpretation."

An official of McGraw-Hill takes the position that it "is a good thing to have the Mississippi boy reading from the same books used in New York. . . . But to do this," he adds, "it is not always possible to say everything New York or some other state wants you to say.

"There is an analogy," the official says, "between textbook publishing and political parties. We take criticism from the right and left and put it in a form the teachers can use. Parties do the same thing in preparing political platforms."

An official of the American Textbook Publishers Institute says textbooks "have come a long way. Up until ten years ago some texts came out in regional editions – one for each section of the country. . . . It may be that today some publishers are exercising unnecessary caution in publishing their books, but it could be a big financial gamble to do otherwise. I think concessions like calling the Civil War the War Between the States are a small price to pay for doing away with regional editions."

Schools could get better books, says a vice-president of the Macmillan Company, if they would select them on the basis of content. The important questions for a textbook selection committee to ask, the official says, are: "What does the book say?" and "How does the book say it?" Instead, books are adopted by schools all too often because they cost a few pennies less than competing books, or because they have colored pictures, attractive covers and a strong binding.

President William E. Spaulding of Houghton Mifflin believes, however, that the charges which come from pressure groups and the attention publishers are forced to give to answering the charges are the most formidable barriers to better texts.

"I cannot speak . . . for all publishers or for authors," says Spaulding, who, as president of the American Textbook Publishers Institute, led the fight against pressure groups in the early fifties. "But I suspect that many of them will change their books in accordance with taboos so long as they believe that those changes do not actually make a book less sound and effective in its content and teaching than it was before. Call this appeasement if you will, but it seems to me that an argument on that issue is not important here." What is important, Spaulding insists, "is a recognition of the opportunities we are missing so long as our minds and efforts are concentrated on taboos and negative measures of defense against communism."

If the consequences were not so important to the school child, it would be easy to laugh at the turn of events which finds the publisher having to avow again and again that he is not plotting to undermine the free enterprise system. There is an especial irony in the publisher's situation because he himself is one of the system's most competitive parts. To believe that he would willingly work to undermine our capitalist economy is to believe that he wants to commit financial suicide.

12

The Choice

DURING the early fifties, when much of the character of today's attacks on textbooks was being shaped, William E. Spaulding, who was then serving as president of the American Textbook Publishers Institute, began looking for a way to cushion textbooks from controversy. He came up with what he and many publishers and educators believed to be an answer. Had it been acted on, publishers might be producing better books today with little hindrance.

What Spaulding proposed was this: *"We can meet the charges which threaten textbooks and education only by substituting understanding for misunderstanding when it exists."*

"There is nothing to be gained," he added, "by blaming the present situation on the small but highly organized group of professional agitators who have sold a phony bill of goods to the American public. Lash back at them as hard as you please, but the fact will remain that for lack of understanding large segments of the American public have accepted their program in the name of patriotism and as one means of defense against communism."

Spaulding's solution to the problem recognizes that citizens have the right, even the duty, to interest themselves in the public schools and the instructional material used in the classroom. There is no way, nor should there be, of preventing them from criticizing anything about the school system they finance with their taxes.

But the citizen also has the right to expect from his press, his educators, and community leaders a clear assessment of what is involved in censorship. The issue, of course, is whether textbooks and therefore the minds of the students, are to be governed by pressure groups or by informed scholars.

Before society can choose, however, it must be given the facts both about the pressure groups which attack the textbooks and the publishers, scholars, educators and teachers who prepare and use them. It is here that the defenders of scholarly texts have failed. The principal national efforts to substitute "understanding for misunderstanding" have come from two organizations: The Commission on Professional Rights and Responsibilities of the National Education Association, the American Textbook Publishers Institute (and, in the case of library books, the American Library Association).

The American Textbook Publishers Institute, for its part, points out that the various screening processes a text must pass through makes it highly unlikely, if not impossible, for a subversive book to reach the child. The average textbook manuscript is examined by qualified editors, a teacher, a scholar and an expert on teaching methods before going to the printing presses. After publication it must then pass hundreds of state and local selection committees. Finally, if it is widely adopted, it will be examined by countless teachers, any one of whom could expose any attempt at indoctrinating the children along collectivist lines.

The Publishers Institute, while having no objection to further screening by parent and citizen groups, urged that books always be scrutinized with five questions in mind:

1. What is the date of the copyright? Books inevitably reflect the intellectual and emotional climate of the time when they are written. A volume written during World War II might treat Russia, for example, in a way markedly different from the one its author would use now.

2. Is the material criticized unfairly? Does the critic understand exactly what subject the book is supposed to cover? Frequently pressure groups criticize a United States history text for failing to cover a subject that is discussed in world history texts.

3. Is the material in question removed from context? To judge fairly, the whole teaching unit must be considered, not merely isolated sentences or paragraphs.

4. When considered with the full content of the book, what effect is the material likely to have on the pupil? Will it be harmful, or will it help the student achieve necessary insight into modern problems and events?

5. How is the material intended to be used in the schools? Is the student taught to accept unthinkingly everything he reads, or is he taught to evaluate and discriminate?

The Commission on Professional Rights and Responsibilities of the NEA provides a service unavailable anywhere else. It compiles and distributes detailed reports on the groups and individuals who try to influence the content of textbooks. When E. Merrill Root's book *Brainwashing in the High Schools* appeared, the commission published a bulletin giving both an analysis of the volume together with a list of Root's organizational affiliations. Another bulletin described the textbook-reviewing methods of America's Future, Inc., pointing out that they were initiated by Lucille Cardin Crain, whose earlier attacks on texts had drawn the attention of a congressional investigation committee. The commission also compiled reports on many of the reviewers of America's Future and showed that most had identified themselves with right-wing causes – a point that while not objectionable in itself hardly qualified them as dispassionate or impartial judges of what children should read.

In addition to the bulletins it issues on textbook censorship, the commission keeps files on almost every textbook controversy which comes to its attention. By studying the patterns of attack used in textbook fights, Dr. Richard Kennan and Dr. Edwin Davis of the commission are often able to detect at a glance which pressure group is working behind the scenes in a specific controversy.

The campaign against textbook censorship was weakened in 1959 when the National Citizens Commission for the Public Schools disbanded. Founded in 1949 through the efforts of Dr. James B. Conant, who was then president of Harvard, and Roy E. Larsen, president of Time, Inc., the commission worked for a decade to acquaint the public with how a textbook is produced and used. The commission approached the problem by frankly admitting that books cannot be perfect: "Textbooks cannot be exclusively factual or entirely objective. Authors, being human, will discuss American institutions with varying degrees of approval and criticism. They are influenced by the climate of opinion at the time they are writing and by their own personal limitations." Nevertheless, the commission insisted, books "should be criticized on the basis of *their merits* and not on the basis of *our prejudices.*"

The NEA commission, the Publishers Institute, and the National Citizens Commission, when it was operating, have done much to put textbook censorship in proper perspective. But there is a limit to what such groups can accomplish – especially when their primary means of disseminating information is restricted to the mails and to public speeches.

The failure of the nation's communications media – the press, radio and television – to give full reports on textbook controversies and pressure groups has permitted censorship activities to flourish with little organized opposition. Three and a half years after the Daughters of the American Revolution launched its campaign against one hundred and seventy textbooks, the fact that the drive was in progress had not been reported to a national audience. The organizations which want to dictate what a book should say about minority and religious groups have received some attention – but only a little.

In too many communities, newspapers have merely reported that a fight over textbooks is under way. They relate the charges made by the would-be censors and a reply or two from a harassed school superintendent or principal. Rarely do they supply the reader with enough facts about the group bringing the charges to allow him to decide whether the group is interested in a fair, impartial, and accurate presentation or in furthering its own views and beliefs. More rarely yet does a newspaper send a reporter to a nearby college to ask competent scholars for a dispassionate analysis of the books and authors under attack.

An exception, however, to the rule of newspaper apathy was the coverage given by the two papers in Meriden, Connecticut, the *Journal* and *Record,* when textbooks were assailed there. During the month in which the controversy was at its peak, the two newspapers ran twenty stories on textbooks, some of the articles filling a column or more. Among other things, reporters sought comment on the "controversial" volumes from recognized authorities at Yale and Wesleyan. One of the editors, Sanford H. Wendover of the *Journal,* examined most of the books in preparing editorials. The result was an informed public; and the informed public in turn made clear its disapproval of the attempts to tamper with the books in use in Meriden schools.

In contrast, only one paper in Texas, the weekly *Texas Observer,* provided its readers with consistent, detailed coverage of censorship fights in that state. Although propaganda from the Daughters of the American Revolution, America's Future, Inc., and other pressure groups figured in the controversy, the extent of their activities – and the criteria they used in judging the books – were never fully reported.

In Mississippi, many newspapers even went so far as to identify E. Merrill Root as an "expert" on textbooks and subversion. They failed to point out that while the books he attacked were texts in history and social studies, he himself had no academic credentials as an historian or political scientist. He was a professor of English literature. In addition, he had belonged to several ultra-conservative organizations and was a reviewer for America's Future, Inc.

If newspapers, television and radio can be called delinquent in their responsibilities, so can many school administrators, teachers, and publishers.

Many of the publishers support the work of the American Textbook Publishers Institute, but there has been a noticeable lack of cooperation among them in meeting the attacks during a specific controversy. In the early stages of the Texas fight, D. C. Heath and Company sent letters to dozens of publishing firms suggesting that they work together to combat the criticism. Only a few publishers approved the idea; several did not answer the letter; and most took the position that "the less said, the better." In some instances, book salesmen have taken advantage of unfounded attacks on a competitor's texts to increase the sales of their own firm's publications.

Despite the efforts of the NEA, the Publishers Institute and the National Citizens Commission to inform them, too many teachers and school administrators remain ignorant of the pressure groups and the methods they use in attempting to censor a text. In the belief that "an attack could never occur in my town," school administrators seldom prepare themselves for criticism until they are actually involved in controversy. It is impossible to determine how often a sincerely troubled parent, brandishing an America's Future review or a DAR report, has met with an educator and left without learning anything about the textbook-reviewing program of either organization. But the success of both groups in campaigning against textbooks indicates it has happened frequently.

Most textbook controversies would collapse in their infancy, the National Education Association says, if school officials and teachers were to follow a simple set of rules:

—"Be alert for the beginning phases of a textbook investigation.

—"Insist that the charges be specific and that they be made in writing.

—"Convince the administration and the board of education that, as the teachers who use the books, you are vitally concerned, you are willing to work on the problem and you have a specialized knowledge needed to meet the situation.

—"Notify your national professional organizations of the situation arising in your community and keep them informed of its progress.

—"Analyze the problem from the standpoint of its pattern, motivation, logic and methods.

—"Do everything you possibly can to see to it that the books in question are thoroughly read and studied in their entirety.

—"Invite those bringing the charges to visit extensively in your classroom.

—"Leave no stone unturned to insure that both sides get a fair hearing.

—"Avoid, as you would the plague, the use of name-calling, flag-waving, glittering generalities, card-stacking and other propaganda devices.

—"See the situation through. 'Staying power,' as contrasted with 'straw-fire' enthusiasm, is called for.

—"Use the incident to take stock of how good a job you are doing in your school."

While substituting understanding for misunderstanding may be the best way to reduce the number of attacks on textbooks, it is a long-range, time-consuming solution. Meanwhile, what can be done to render the attacks ineffective?

One answer is for concerned citizens to insist that scholarly judgment – and not the protests of pressure groups – be the guide in determining what is put in or left out of a textbook. Another possible approach, but one which has its opponents and its pitfalls, is for states to abolish centralized textbook selection committees and allow each school district to select the books it wants to use in its schools.

In 1962 there was a hodgepodge of textbook selection methods in use in the United States. In Alabama and North Carolina (and in California at the elementary-school level), one committee selected a basic text to be used statewide in each subject in each school. In seventeen other states, local school systems could use only those books which had been placed on an "approved list" by a state committee. (Approved lists generally consist of from three to ten book titles.)

The "approved list" method of textbook selection is called "multiple adoption" and was used in 1962 by Alaska, Florida, Georgia, Idaho, Indiana, Kentucky, Louisiana, Mississippi, Nevada, New Mexico, Oklahoma, Oregon, South Carolina, Tennessee, Utah, Texas and Virginia. West Virginia, Arizona and Arkansas also use the plan in choosing texts for elementary schools, but leave the choice of high-school texts to the local school systems.

All other states leave textbook selection entirely to the localities – a practice favored by almost every publisher. "Publishers almost never yield to pressure from a state where textbook selection is up to the local schools," says a McGraw-Hill vice-president. "There usually is not enough business from any one city or one county to make it worthwhile. But you are going to think a long time before refusing to make a change requested by a committee that can keep you from selling your books in an entire state."

Other publishers point out that their authors would write more freely if central committees did not screen the books. "As long as a single committee in Mississippi can keep your book from being sold there," says one book editor, "you are going to watch what you say about segregation and integration."

Many educators have joined the publishers in opposing book selection at the state level. "Most people in the education business believe it is best to allow as much leeway as possible in the selection of books," says Dr. John H. Fischer, dean of Columbia Teachers College. Dr. Francis Keppel, dean of the Harvard Graduate School of Education, says diffusion of responsibility through local selection is a safeguard against bigotry creeping into adoption procedures. "If you have a lot of people choosing from a wide list there is less chance of any one set of views being imposed," Keppel says.

There are other educators, however, who are wary of plans for putting textbook adoption entirely into local hands. They contend that a state textbook committee which is both competent and free from political pressure can often keep the worst textbooks out of a state. You might eliminate changes, such as those that were made in Texas, by abolishing state textbook committees, say opponents of local adoption, but you might leave the way open for more communities to supply their children with out-of-date volumes like the McGuffey Readers. In addition, they argue, a small school system might be overburdened if it had to listen to every textbook publisher who wanted to demonstrate his books.

While decentralized book selection might mitigate the

effects of censorship campaigns, the ultimate answer to the textbook problem depends upon public insistence that scholars, and not pressure groups, decide what is to be in a textbook. And there are indications that many parents, alarmed at the progress Russia is making in education, are beginning to insist that their children be given only the best instructional material.

Fred M. Hechinger, the education editor of the New York *Times,* studied the textbook problem in early 1962 and reported the beginnings of a revolution in the textbook industry. "The textbook publishing industry today is in a position comparable to that of the aircraft industry when it was confronted by the changeover from piston engines to jets," says Hechinger. "Demands for higher standards of teaching have caused textbook innovations, that according to one publisher, might normally have taken at least a generation."

But most of the changes have taken place in biology, chemistry, math, language and physics texts, Hechinger says. Texts for courses in economics, elementary reading, literature, history, government and geography have not kept pace with those produced for the sciences.

Still, says Hechinger, publishers of books used in the "humanities" are finding themselves caught in a crossfire of criticism, with right-wing groups and segregationists claiming that books are "too liberal" and others contending that the texts have been drained of substance and controversy. Adding to the pressure on the publishers, are the minority and religious groups who want their race or their religion treated in a more favorable light.

As Hechinger points out, a struggle is under way. It is too soon to predict the outcome, but not to warn of the consequences if the pressure groups continue to carry the day.

"It is one thing to express honest criticism of some school text or teaching program and raise public questions about it," says the Winston-Salem, North Carolina, *Journal.* "It is quite another thing to use group pressure to have certain materials banned because they do not conform to some special group's ideas about Americanism, minority group interests, or whatnot.

"If we allow pressure groups, rather than our qualified educators, to determine the content of school books, teaching in our schools will soon degenerate into indoctrination, with facts being embroidered with propaganda and truth tailored to fit some super-zealots' pet prejudice or theory. Then we will have a school system on a par with that of Hitler's Nazi Germany or those of Soviet Russia and Red China."

The prospect, to say the least, is a forbidding one.

Bibliography

BOOKS

Beale, Howard K. *Are American Teachers Free?* New York: Scribner's, 1936.

———. *A History of Freedom of Teaching in American Schools.* New York: Scribner's, 1941.

Blanshard, Paul. *The Right to Read.* Boston: Beacon Press, 1955.

Cronbach, Lee J., editor. *Text Materials in Modern Education.* Urbana: University of Illinois Press, 1955.

Davis, Wallace Evan. *Patriotism on Parade.* Cambridge: Harvard University Press, 1955.

Education Policies Commission of the National Education Association. *The Education of Free Men.* Washington: NEA, 1941.

Forster, Arnold. *A Measure of Freedom.* New York: Doubleday, 1950.

———, and Benjamin Epstein. *The Troublemakers.* New York: Doubleday, 1952.

Luthin, Reinhard H. *American Demagogues.* Boston: Beacon Press, 1954.

Marcus, Lloyd. *The Treatment of Minorities in Secondary School Textbooks.* New York: Anti-Defamation League of B'nai B'rith, 1961.

McKeon, Richard, and others, *The Freedom to Read.* New York: R. R. Bowker Company, 1957.

Pierce, Bessie Louise. *Citizens Organizations and the Civic Training of Youth.* New York: Scribner's, 1933.

———. *Public Opinion and the Teaching of History in the U. S.* New York: Alfred A. Knopf, 1926.

Root, E. Merrill. *Brainwashing in the High Schools.* New York: Devin-Adair, 1958.

———. *Collectivism on the Campus.* New York: Devin-Adair, 1954.

Roy, Ralph Lord. *Apostles of Discord.* Boston: Beacon Press, 1953.

Rudd, Augustin G. *Bending the Twig.* Chicago: Heritage Foundation, 1957.

Rugg, Harold. *That Men May Understand.* New York: Doubleday, 1951.

Schriftgiesser, Karl. *The Lobbyists.* Boston: Atlantic–Little, Brown, 1951.

NEWSPAPERS

Amarillo (Tex.) *Daily News,* Mar. 1, 1962.

Amarillo *Globe-Times,* Jan. 26, Jan. 28, 1962.

Atlanta (Ga.) *Constitution,* July 6, Sept. 5, Oct. 3, Nov. 24, 1951; May 2, 1955; Sept. 7, Sept. 22, 1961.

Atlanta *Journal,* Sept. 27, Sept. 29, Oct. 13, 1950; Jan. 3, June 28, Sept. 20, Oct. 28, Nov. 23, 1951; Mar. 16, Apr. 24, Aug. 13, 1952; Jan. 15, 1953.

Austin (Tex.) *American,* Nov. 6, 1936; Apr. 29, Dec. 9, 1961.

Austin *Statesman,* Feb. 25, 1959.

Austin *Texas Observer,* Jan. 26, Sept. 22, Oct. 6, Dec. 8, 1961; Jan. 19, Feb. 2, Mar. 2, 1962.

Boston *Christian Science Monitor,* Dec. 1, 1961.

Boston *Herald,* Aug. 29, 1960.

Charlotte (N.C.) *Observer,* May 5, 1959.

Dallas (Tex.) *News,* June 10, 1956; Jan. 25, 1960.

Dallas *Times-Herald,* Jan. 31, 1960.

Dayton (Ohio) *Daily News,* Feb. 23, 1941; Sept. 12, 1957.

Evanston (Ill.) *Review,* Nov. 13, 1958.

Fresno (Cal.) *Bee,* May 8, 1957.

Grand Rapids (Mich.) *Press,* Feb. 22, 1962.

Hartford (Conn.) *Courant,* Dec. 20, 1961.

Houston (Tex.) *Chronicle,* Jan. 4, 1959; Jan. 28, 1962.
Los Angeles (Cal.) *Herald and Express* (now the *Herald-Examiner),* Nov. 6-11, Dec. 11-12, 1961; Jan. 1-3, 1962.
Los Angeles *Mirror News,* June 29, 1960.
Los Angeles *Times,* Jan. 13, 1962.
Meriden (Conn.) *Journal,* files, especially for Nov. and Dec., 1961, and Jan., 1962.
Meriden *Record,* files, especially for Nov. and Dec., 1961, and Jan., 1962.
Miami (Fla.) *Herald,* Apr. 7, 1960; Apr. 4, Apr. 23, 1962.
Nashville *Tennessean,* Jan. 31, 1953.
New York *Times,* Feb. 23, 1941; Sept. 12, 1957; Mar. 28, 1960; May 18, 1961; Apr. 5, 1962.
New York *World-Telegram,* Aug. 25, 1948.
Palm Beach (Fla.) *Times,* June 4, 1959.
Pawtucket (R.I.) *Times.*
Philadelphia *Bulletin,* Nov. 12, 1961.
Raleigh (N.C.) *News and Observer,* textbook files.
Santa Ana (Cal.) *Register,* May 5, 1957.
San Angelo (Cal.) *Standard-Times,* Feb. 1, 1962.
San Antonio (Tex.) *Express,* Sept. 27, 1936.

PERIODICALS

Alexander, A. "The Gray Flannel Cover on the American History Textbook." *Social Education,* January, 1960.
American Mercury, January, 1960.
American Opinion, 1958–1962.
Amherst Alumni News, January, 1959.
Armstrong, O. K. "Treason in the Textbooks." *American Legion Magazine,* September, 1940.
Bainbridge, John. "Dangers Ahead in the Public Schools." *McCall's,* October, 1952.
Cassels, Louis. "The Rightist Crisis in Our Churches." *Look,* April 24, 1962.
Christian Crusade Magazine, June, 1961.
DAR Magazine, November, 1957.

Educational Reviewer, several issues, especially July, 1949, and January 15, 1953.

Esbensen, T. "How Far Have the Book Burners Gone?" *School Executive,* May, 1957.

Freedom Facts, November, 1957.

Haefner, J. F. "Battle of the Books." *NEA Journal,* April, 1953.

Hamburg, M. "Case of the Subversive Text." *School Executive,* April, 1958.

Hechinger, Fred M. "A Summing Up." *Saturday Review,* April 19, 1952.

Human Events, July 30, 1952.

Knowlton, P. A. "What is Wrong With Textbooks? – Confessions of a School Book Publisher." *School Executive,* October, 1950.

Krug, Mark M. "Safe Textbooks and Citizenship Education." *School Review,* Winter, 1960.

Martin, Harold H. "Doomsday Merchant on the Far, Far Right." *Saturday Evening Post,* April 28, 1962.

Matthews, J. B. "Reds in our Churches." *American Mercury,* July, 1953.

Mayer, Martin. "The Trouble with Textbooks." *Harper's,* July, 1962.

McCaffrey, Austin J. "Should Textbooks Take a Stand?" *Senior Scholastic,* November, 1960.

Morse, Arthur D. "Who's Trying to Ruin Our Schools?" *McCall's,* September, 1951.

NEA Journal, February, 1962.

New Republic. "A Special Report on the Censorship of Books," 1953.

New Republic, September 9, 1936.

Newsweek, January 2, 1961; September 10, 1956.

Publishers' Weekly, April 24, 1954; October 2, 1961; October 23, 1961.

Saveth, Edward N. "What to Do About Dangerous Textbooks." *Commentary,* February, 1952.

Serviss, T. K. "Freedom to Learn – Censorship in Learning Materials." *Social Education,* February, 1953.

Shaplen, Robert. "Scarsdale's Battle of the Books." *Commentary,* December, 1950.

Social Education, March, 1959.

Spaulding, W. E. "Can Textbooks Be Subversive?" *Education Digest,* October, 1953.

Stillwell, Clara. "America's Schoolbook Scandal." *Christian Herald,* September, 1950.

Time, May 16, 1960; July 10, 1939; March 3, 1941; May 9, 1960.

PAMPHLETS AND REPORTS

American Book Publishers Council, Inc. Freedom-To-Read Bulletins and censorship bulletins.

America's Future, Inc. *Nine Men Against America,* by Rosalie M. Gordon.

———. *What's Happened to Our Schools?,* by Rosalie M. Gordon.

———. Copy of cover letter from Robert F. Montgomery, CPA, to America's Future, Inc., with copy of America's Future's statement of assets and liabilities as of December, 1961.

California. Document containing revisions suggested by the State Curriculum Commission in fiifth- and eighth-grade social studies textbooks.

Casey, Edward M., and Frederick H. Dobson. "Citizens' Report on Social Science Textbooks in the Meriden Public Schools."

Daughters of the American Revolution. *Textbook Study.*

Florida Coalition of Patriotic Societies. Miscellaneous material.

Harding College. *The National Program.*

Hirshfield, David. A report on investigation of pro-British history textbooks in use in the public schools in the city of New York, published at the direction of New York Mayor John F. Hylan, 1923.

Institute of Special Research, Pasadena, California. *The Left Swing in Public Education.*

National Council for American Education, New York. *Private School: The Solution to America's Educational Problem.*

National Council of the Churches of Christ in the U.S.A., New York. *The Truth.*

National Education Association. Defense bulletins and information bulletins.

National Research Bureau, Chicago. Pamphlets.

The Parents for Better Education, Los Angeles. Miscellaneous pamphlets and material.

Sons of the American Revolution. *A Bill of Grievances.*

Texas Education Agency. Report of the State Textbook Committee to the State Commissioner of Education on books offered for adoption 1961; Transcript of proceedings at State Textbook Committee hearing, September, 1961.

The Veterans of Foreign Wars of the United States. *Treason to American Tradition,* by Charles Grant Miller, 1922.

We the People! Pamphlets.

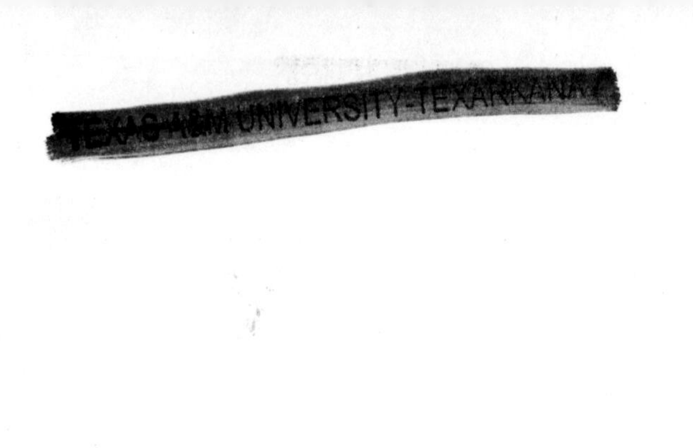
TEXAS A&M UNIVERSITY-TEXARKANA